Alfred Williams

The Inter-Oceanic Canal and the Monroe Doctrine

Alfred Williams

The Inter-Oceanic Canal and the Monroe Doctrine

ISBN/EAN: 9783337034542

Printed in Europe, USA, Canada, Australia, Japan

Cover: Foto ©Thomas Meinert / pixelio.de

More available books at **www.hansebooks.com**

THE

INTER-OCEANIC CANAL

AND

THE MONROE DOCTRINE.

"AT AN EPOCH WHICH WE MAY CALL NEAR, SINCE IT CONCERNS THE LIFE OF A PEOPLE, THE ANGLO-AMERICANS WILL COVER ALL THE IMMENSE TERRITORY COMPRISED BETWEEN THE POLAR ICE AND THE TROPICS—THEY WILL SPREAD FROM THE SHORES OF THE ATLANTIC OCEAN EVEN TO THE COASTS OF THE SOUTHERN SEA."

DE TOCQUEVILLE.

NEW YORK :

G. P. PUTNAM'S SONS,

182 FIFTH AVENUE.

1880.

CONTENTS.

INTRODUCTION.

THE appearance upon the Isthmus of Darien, at the outset of the year 1880, of M. Ferdinand de Lesseps, the renowned French engineer and diplomatist, to whom the nineteenth century owes the inception and completion of the Suez Canal, has startled the thinking people of this country into a sudden but most desirable state of anxiety as to the effects likely to be produced upon the interests, the prestige, and the prosperity of the United States by the opening, under other auspices than ours, of a great waterway between the Atlantic and the Pacific oceans. Though the question of opening such a waterway has occupied the minds of American statesmen and of American engineers at intervals, ever since the foundation of the republic, and though it has of late years acquired an unprecedented gravity and importance for the American people, through the establishment of our vast empire on the Pacific, and the immense development of our internal railway system between the Great Lakes and the Gulf, it has been so much obscured by exciting domestic issues, now happily coming to an end, that for Americans of the present generation it may be treated as a question almost absolutely new. It cannot be intelligently considered without quickening the enlightened patriotism of the American people, by making it more than ever apparent how vitally important it is to the prosperity of every State and every section of our beloved Union, that the primacy and predominance on this continent of the united republic should be jealously guarded against invasion from any quarter, no matter under what pretext or in what form attempted.

In considering this question, as in considering all questions which arise out of or affect the relations between the United States and the powers of Europe, it must always be borne in mind that but little more than fifty years have elapsed since the United States took their place definitely in the system of Christendom as a power to be "counted with," to be considered, and to be respected. As we shall hereafter see, it was not until the ministers of the Holy Alliance, after the death at St. Helena of Napoleon I., had undertaken to consolidate throughout the world the system of government by divine right, that England, in her own interest quite as much as in the interests of liberty, called upon the government of the United States to proclaim the close on this continent of the period of European colonial experiments. The response of the American government to that call gave birth to what has 'ever since been known as the Monroe doctrine; and the unyielding assertion of that doctrine against every attempt to evade or to impair its force has ever since, with reason, been regarded by American statesmen of all' shades of political opinion as essential to the position, the prestige, and the prosperity of the United States.

It will be shown in the course of this treatise that any attempt to construct an inter-oceanic canal between the Atlantic and the Pacific, under European auspices and with European capital, must inevitably lead to a very serious invasion of the position, to a very serious assault upon the prestige, and to very mischievous consequences to the prosperity of the United States. Had any one or more of the independent republics, called into existence by the disruption and destruction, during the first quarter of this century, of the vast American empire of Spain, acquired strength and stability enough to make the construction possible of an inter-oceanic canal through Spanish - American territory by Spanish-

8   *THE INTER-OCEANIC CANAL.*

American citizens with Spanish-American funds, all
that it would be seemly or necessary for the government of the United States to do in regard to such a
canal, doubtless, might be shown to be that it should
secure for the citizens and the commerce of the
United States the free and unrestricted use of the
facilities of such a canal, on at least equal terms
with the citizens and the commerce of all other nations. But no one pretends that this is the case;
and the conditions under which alone any canal enterprise either has been attempted, or is likely to
be attempted in our time by European capitalists in
Spanish America, involve the virtual surrender to
such capitalists, or to the governments of the countries to which they may belong, of the independence
of the State or of the States through the territory of
which the canal projected is to be carried. In other
words, no canal enterprise in Spanish-American territory can be planned, organized, and carried out by
European projectors and capitalists, without practically reopening on this continent that period of
European colonial experiments which the United
States, under President Monroe, distinctly and sol-
emnly declared to be closed forever. It is vital to
our greatness, and our honor as a nation, that this
declaration shall be maintained. We do not doubt
that it will be so maintained, at any cost, by the
people of the United States.

━ The idea of opening a waterway from the Atlantic, the ocean of Europe, to the great Southern Sea, the ocean of Asia, of "Ormus and of Ind," may be said to be coeval with the earliest enterprises of European colonization in the New World. It was in quest of such a waterway that Columbus sailed from Palos in 1492 ; and Cortez planned the construction of such a waterway during his visit to the Isthmus of Tehuantepec, forty years afterward. The "Secret of the Strait," was the goad which drove so many seamen from all the lands of Europe westward through all the earlier years of the sixteenth century, till Magellan found an answer to it far to the stormy south.

The idea of facilitating commercial intercourse between Europe and the East by means of a canal across the Isthmus of Suez, had occurred ages before to the Greek rulers of Egypt, and the statement is reasonably well authenticated that a small canal was made across that isthmus about 600 years B.C., and remained in use until about the year A.D. 800. The history of that ancient work, however, is so obscure that we are without any data for determining with any accuracy how much the commerce of antiquity may have been modified and benefited by the first Suez Canal. It is certain, however, that with the rise of the Turkish and the Saracenic power it ceased to be available to Europe, and when, in the fifteenth century, Venice and other States on the Mediterranean were seeking to extend their commerce in all directions, the discovery of a route by water to the Indies was made a matter of supreme importance to them by the menacing growth of the Ottoman Empire. By the middle of the fifteenth century too, learned and thoughtful men had reasoned out the theory of the spherical form of the earth.

Luigi Pulci, the Florentine poet, as early as 1487, wrote:

> "Men shall descry another hemisphere,
> " Since to one common center all things tend ;
> " So Earth by curious mystery divine
> " Well balanced hangs amid the starry spheres.
>
> " At our antipodes are cities, states,
> " And thronged empires, ne'er divined of yore.
> " But see, the sun speeds on his western path
> " To glad the nations with expected light."

Five years later, the discovery of a continent beyond the western ocean by Columbus startled the world almost simultaneously with the discovery of the Cape of Good Hope, by Vasco da Gama, and the dreams of the poet became the facts of the geographer.

The last voyage of Columbus was undertaken expressly to find the strait into the Asian seas. After much suffering he reached the coast of Honduras, along which he sought in vain a passage to the East.

It was an unsuccessful enterprise, but there is satisfaction in the thought that in that last voyage, near the sad close of his eventful life, he sailed along the shores of the isthmus through which, pierced as it surely will be by a ship canal, the commerce of Europe with Asia will at last, and in part at least, be interchanged.

The Spanish navigators after Columbus kept up an active search for a shorter route to the Indies. "This discovery of a strait into the Indian Ocean," says Prescott, "was the burden of every order from the government." The discovery of a new route to India, "is the true key to the maritime movements of the fifteenth and the first half of the sixteenth centuries."

One of the most important results of these Spanish explorations was the discovery of the Pacific Ocean in 1513, by the unfortunate Balboa. Geographical researches soon satisfied the Spaniards that no natural inter-oceanic water channel existed in those regions in which they had so diligently sought "the secret of the Strait." Their voyages, and those made by contemporary Portuguese and English navigators, gradually gave Europeans some elementary knowledge of both the Eastern and Western continents. It was then seen that although all the regions of the earth which, on account of their wealth and population, afforded the

best materials for commerce, lay within the Northern Hemisphere, direct intercourse by water between
many of the richest of these countries was cut off by
the projection of South America and Africa far beyond the equator. The narrow isthmuses by which
these two continents were joined to their northern
neighbors soon suggested, however, the practicability of piercing those obstructions by means of artificial water channels.

Even before the contemporaries of Columbus had
all passed away, the longing for the rich fruits of
Eastern commerce had distinctly presented to the
attention of mankind the problem of an American
inter-oceanic canal—a problem which has, says Sumner, "not only a practical value, but an historic
grandeur"—a problem which, after the lapse of more
than three centuries, remains unsolved.

The Spaniards are entitled to the credit of having
at a very early day formed the project of uniting
the harbors on opposite sides of the American isthmus by means of a canal between the headwaters of
the streams flowing in opposite directions to the
Atlantic and Pacific. As early as 1528, Antonio
Galvao proposed to the Emperor Charles V. to open
a communication between the oceans by the Isthmus
of Panama. During the reign of Philip II., the
authorities even went so far as to make plans and
surveys for carrying an inter-oceanic canal scheme

into execution. But Spain was already growing weak at the extremities of her colossal empire ; the filibusters of England, France, and Holland swarmed in the seas, and Philip forbade the execution of the work. He wanted wisdom to perceive that the control of such an important channel of commerce would have given more strength and durable prosperity to his empire than all the wealth of his mines of gold and silver.

The importance of the Isthmian region, in a commercial point of view, attracted the attention of William Patterson, the founder of the Bank of England, and one of the most remarkable men of his age, toward the end of the seventeenth century, and a canal to be cut through it was one of the objects of his great but ill-fated scheme of the Darien colony. The tragic termination of this project is well known. Lord Macaulay, in his History of England, tells the story in his most graphic style; but although embellished with all the charms of the fascinating rhetoric of this brilliant historian, the narrative shows no adequate recognition of the wisdom and statesmanship displayed in the conception of this colony, and it is not too much to say, that but for the purblind and jealous policy of King William III., Great Britain might have secured through Patterson, in the closing years of the seventeenth century, a colonial possession of more importance than all the wide extended territory which she now owns in North America. Had Patterson's scheme been honestly supported, the British government would have acquired firm possession of the American isthmus, and with that isthmus in her possession, she would, doubtless, long since have constructed an inter-oceanic canal, which might have adjourned for long years to come the construction of the canal of Suez. Never did a nation spurn a gift so precious. The sanction of the British government alone was wanting to insure success to a colonial enterprise which carried with it all the blessings of civilization, and the well-ordered material, moral, and social development of Anglo-Saxon enlightenment —an enterprise which, commencing on the narrow confines of the Isthmus of Darien, and spreading to the neighboring lands of Central and South America, might have resulted in a success more enduring than that of the East India Company. Patterson looked beyond the dominion of the isthmus. His large ambition included the acquisition of Cuba as a part of his comprehensive plan for British supremacy on this hemisphere. His enlightened and sagacious views deserve the consideration of the American people, whose interest in the regions which attracted his enterprising spirit is paramount now to that of any other people. We have an intimation of the wide scope of his entire plan in his own words, as follows:

"The addition of the port of Havana to those ports and passes of the isthmus will render this design altogether complete.

"Havana is capable of being defended with five or six thousand seasoned men ashore, and the situation thereof upon one of the best and greatest islands, not only of America, but may be in the world, as lying in the center between the Northern and Southern parts of America, and thereby making a pass of the greatest consequence, and a natural bridle to all that great inlet commonly called the Gulf, and no small awe to the navigation of the whole bay of Mexico."

The following passage from a letter written by this remarkable man presents a further elucidation of his views:

"But if neither Britain singly, nor the maritime powers of Europe will treat for Darien, the period is not very far distant when, instead of waiting for the slow returns of trade, America will seize the pass of Darien. Their next move will be to hold the Sandwich Islands. Stationed thus in the middle, on the east and on the west sides of the New World, the English-Americans will form the most potent and singular empire that has appeared, because it will consist, not in the dominion of a part of the land of the globe, but in the dominion of the whole ocean. They can make the tour of the Indian and Southern seas, collecting wealth by trade wherever they pass. During European wars, they may have the carrying trade of all. If blessed with letters and arts, they will spread civilization over the Universe. Then England, with all her liberties and glory, may be known only as Egypt is now."

These are instructive, not to say prophetic words, and may be read with profit by every American citizen to-day.

THE COMMERCIAL IMPORTANCE OF THE INTER-OCEANIC CANAL, AND THE HISTORY OF SOME OF THE SCHEMES FOR BUILDING IT.

IT is foreign to the purposes of this treatise to give a detailed history of the numerous schemes devised during the past 350 years for the establishment of inter-oceanic communication across the American isthmus.

A chronological list of the most important of these plans is given in an appendix, but a rapid review of the subject here will show how often and how deservedly it has occupied public attention.

The writings of Humboldt were influential in directing attention to this great work at the beginning of the present century. His personal explorations vividly impressed him with the benefit the commerce of all nations would derive from an inter-oceanic canal; and also with the practicability of the enterprise.

In his work on "New Spain," the relative merits of the Tehuantepec, Nicaragua, Panama, and Atrato routes are carefully discussed, and although of necessity he studied only in the light of such general and unsatisfactory data as could be obtained by an intelligent traveler, unaided in most cases by the surveys of engineers, the elements of the problem are presented with rare intelligence, and the fact that those whose subsequent studies have been most thorough, have the highest admiration for the accuracy of his information and the soundness of his conclusions, is a tribute to the sagacity with which his comprehensive mind grasped the entire subject.

The power of Spain was already completely broken at the time of Humboldt's visit to the isthmus, yet the enlightened Charles III. had seriously revolved the project of constructing a canal during his reign, and Revillagigedo, his not less enlightened Mexican Viceroy, had made explorations to that end. After the American provinces had achieved their independence, public interest in the inter-oceanic canal problem at once revived. Bolivar cherished to the last the hope of solving it in the interest of Colombia. Upon the fall of the Spanish power, and the separation of Guatemala from the ephemeral empire of Iturbide in Mexico, the Nicaraguan scheme was revived by Central America, united under a federal government. The interstate jealousies of the Central American Republic were strong enough, however, to dissolve the union and to suspend all such schemes.

On the 8th of February, 1825, during the closing month of Mr. Monroe's administration, Mr. Canaz, who then represented the Central American Republic at Washington, addressed a note to the Department of State, proposing the co-operation of that republic with the United States in promoting the opening of a canal through the province of Nicaragua ; and proposing also, that by means of a treaty the advantages of the canal should be perpetually secured to the two nations. The note remained unnoticed until after the beginning of the administration of John Quincy Adams, when on the 18th of April, 1825, Mr. Clay, his Secretary of State, replied to it, but without taking any direct notice of the important proposition for a treaty which it contained. Mr. Clay instructed Mr. Williams, then our Minister in Central America, to investigate the Nicaragua route with the greatest care, and to inform the government of the result of his inquiries.

Mr. Williams seems to have taken a deep interest in the subject. Through his influence, on the 16th of June, 1826, a contract was entered into with the Central American government, on behalf of Aaron H. Palmer of New York, for the construction of a canal through Nicaragua, with a capacity for "vessels of the largest burden possible." Mr. Palmer does not appear to have had any reliable information as to the cost of the work, although he had as his associate so judicious a practical engineer as De Witt Clinton, and was assisted by the Marquis Aycinena, a Guatemalan exile of ability.

It was proposed to raise a capital of only $5,000,-000, for the prosecution of the entire work. The scheme failed, owing to the inability of the company which Mr. Palmer represented to raise the amount required.

The American company having failed in the fulfillment of its contract, negotiations were opened by Central America with Holland, which came to a favorable conclusion under the direct patronage of the king in 1830 ; but the commencement of the undertaking by the Dutch company was prevented by the political disturbances which resulted in the independence of Belgium ; and, upon the failure of the Dutch company to carry out the agreement to construct the canal, the people of Central America turned again for aid to the United States, as their natural ally in the work. Mr. Savage, consul of the United States at Guatemala, wrote to the Department of State, on the 3d of December, 1830: "Every one seems tacitly to look forward to the United States for the completion of this grand project. They say that the United States, identified in her institutions with this government, *is the only power that ought to have the preference.*"

The Nicaraguan inter-oceanic canal was one of the first subjects which engaged the attention of Jackson's administration.

On the 20th of July, 1831, Mr. Livingston, Secretary of State, addressed the following instructions to Mr. Jeffers, American Chargé in Central America :

" . . . You will endeavor to procure for the citizens of the United States, *or for the government itself*, if Congress should deem the measure constitutional and proper, the right of subscribing to the stock ; and you will in either case procure and transmit such plans, estimates, and other information relative to the projected work as may enable us to judge of its feasibility and importance. The depth of water, safety from storms, capacity, and other facilities of the projected ports at the two extremities, are particularly important to be known, as well as the intended length, breadth, and depth of the canal itself, and the time calculated for constructing it."

Mr. Jeffers resigned without going to his post, but this extract is exceedingly interesting as showing the views entertained on this subject by the administration of General Jackson, and the readiness of that administration even to make the government a partner in the enterprise.

On the 3d of March, 1835, the Senate of the United States adopted the following resolution :

"*Resolved*, That the President of the United States be respectfully requested to consider the expediency of opening negotiations with the governments of other nations, and particularly with the governments of Central America and New Granada, for the purpose of effectually protecting, by suitable treaty stipulations with them, such individuals or companies as may undertake to open a communication between the Atlantic and Pacific oceans, by construction of a ship canal across the isthmus which connects North and South America, and of securing forever, by such stipulations, the free and equal right of navigating such canal, to all such nations, on the payment of such reasonable tolls as may be established to compensate the capitalists who may engage in such undertaking, to complete the work."

In accordance with this resolution, President Jackson appointed Mr. Charles Biddle, of Philadelphia, a special agent of the government. He was instructed to proceed immediately to Port San Juan, to ascend the river San Juan to the Lake of Nicaragua, and thence by the contemplated route of communication by canal or railroad to the Pacific Ocean. After having examined the route, he was to repair to the capital of Central America, and procure all the documents to be had, relating to the subject. Mr. Biddle was also instructed to make inquiries in regard to the Panama route, but this branch of the subject was subordinate to the main purpose of his mission.

Mr. Biddle, disobeying his instructions, sailed to Panama, alleging that he could not obtain conveyance to San Juan, and from Panama proceeded to Bogota, where he opened negotiations with New Granada for a macadamized road across the Isthmus of Panama.

Having succeeded in obtaining a grant for this purpose, in which he seems to have had a large personal interest, he returned to the United States. His course did not meet the approval of the government, and his project proved a failure.

The first actual survey of a canal route across the State of Nicaragua seems to have been that begun in 1837 by Lieut. John Baily, R.M., who was employed for this purpose by the Federal Government of Central America, a short time previous to its dissolution. Mr. Baily was an officer of the British Royal Marines, who had resided for thirty years in Nicaragua. He was fully competent to the undertaking, and in the two years devoted to the survey he accomplished much that has permanent value. General Morazan undertook to raise a loan in Europe upon the faith of Mr. Baily's surveys, but his design was frustrated by the overthrow of the Federal

Government, the flight of Morazan into Costa Rica, and his execution there.

The subject still continued to engage attention in the United States, and in 1839, the House of Representatives, on the memorial of a number of leading merchants of Philadelphia and New York, adopted a resolution requesting the President to consider the expediency of negotiating with other nations "for the purpose of ascertaining the practicability of effecting a communication between the Atlantic and Pacific oceans, by the construction of a ship canal across the isthmus, and of securing forever, by suitable treaty stipulations, the *free and equal right of navigating such canal to all nations.*" It does not appear that any governmental action followed this resolution.

The Nicaragua route did not, for several years after this period, receive much consideration, owing chiefly to the disturbed political condition of the severed States which had formerly constituted the Central American Republic. In 1844, M. Castellon, of Nicaragua, visited France for the purpose of interesting the government of Louis Philippe in the subject, but he found the Prime Minister, M. Guizot, committed to the Panama route, which Garella was then engaged in examining. Louis Napoleon was then imprisoned at Ham, for his attempt to revolutionize the government of France, and the authorities, willing to find employment for this troublesome prisoner, permitted him to have an interview with Castellon. So far as appears, no definite arrangements were made for his release, although he pledged himself to undertake the work if permitted to go to America.

Nicaragua showed her willingness to place him at the head of the enterprise, by granting a charter, in 1846, to the "*Canal Napoleon de Nicaragua.*" Soon after Napoleon's subsequent escape from prison, he published in London a pamphlet entitled "Canal de Nicaragua," with an appeal to capitalists on behalf of the enterprise. It has never been known in this country how far toward success the canal scheme of Prince Louis Napoleon had been pushed, when the revolution of February, 1848, called him away from the work to overthrow a republic and to found the Second Empire. It may be well now to say that the necessary funds were assured, that the arrangements for commencing the work were in progress, and that the English operations in Central America which roused the indignation of this country, and eventually led to the too cele-brated Clayton-Bulwer negotiations, were under-taken in connection with the development of the Napoleonic scheme.

The acquisition of California by the American government, and the discovery of gold there soon afterward, gave a greater prominence than ever before to the subject of inter-oceanic communication. The necessity for immediate means of transit for the large emigration to California rendered imperative the adoption of temporary expedients for the transit of the isthmus, and led to the opening of an overland route by the Isthmus of Panama, and to another across the Isthmus of Nicaragua, by the San Juan River and the lake in part, and by land from the lake to the Pacific.

Surveys and explorations were immediately commenced upon both routes. In this connection, the labors of Frederick M. Kelley deserve to be mentioned with the highest praise. He devoted his fortune and his time to the investigation of the problem of the discovery of a practicable canal route. It is not within the scope of this work to give a detailed account of the causes which rendered the labors of Kelley and his contemporaries futile. So far as the Isthmus of Panama is concerned, the explorations and surveys resulted in the construction of the Panama Railroad, which was commenced in 1850, at a cost of $7,500,000, by a company chartered by the State of New York, and protected by treaty stipulations between the Colombian and American governments.

The construction of this railroad was a memorable achievement of human energy, and has made famous the names of our countrymen, Aspinwall, Stephens, and Totten, by whose perseverance and zeal the enterprise was carried to a successful conclusion.

Even after the suspension of the projects of Louis Napoleon, the prospects of the Nicaragua inter-oceanic canal seemed good. The work was taken in hand by the Browns of New York, and on the 27th August, 1849, a contract for constructing a canal was entered into by a New York company, called the American Atlantic and Pacific Ship Canal Company. O. W. Childs, a distinguished engineer of Philadelphia, employed by the company to make a thorough survey of the route, began the work in August, 1850. His survey, the most careful and scientific made to that date, was, at the request of the company, referred, by Mr. Conrad, Secretary of War, to Colonel J. J. Abert and Major W. Turnbull, of the United States Topographical Engineers, who pronounced the plan practicable, and expressed the opinion that no other route is so well supplied with water as that through Nicaragua.

The plans submitted by Childs did not, however, meet the approval of capitalists, chiefly because the size of the canal proposed by him was not deemed sufficient for the wants of commerce. The failure of the American Atlantic and Pacific Canal Company to undertake the construction of a canal, was really due to the fact that a subordinate company, formed

by it, and known as the Accessory Transit Company,
found the business of carrying passengers and treasure across the isthmus so profitable, that it was interested in postponing the construction of the canal.
The project was finally ruined by the Walker expedition, and the consequent prejudice and animosity
which that ill-fated adventurer stirred up in Nicaragua against the American people.

The events of 1861, in the United States, put an
end to all attempts on the part of American citizens
to construct the Nicaragua inter-oceanic canal.

Three years before that time, however, Louis Napoleon, become Emperor of the French, had given
the world a signal illustration of the tenacity with
which he clung to his favorite idea of utilizing the
canal project to re-establish French influence in the
New World.   Under his protection, and with direct
encouragement from him, M. Felix Belly, an engineer of ability, and a man full of energy and enthusiasm, organized, in 1858, a company to construct a
canal by way of the San Juan. He obtained con-
tracts both from Costa Rica and from Nicaragua,
and, accompanied by a number of workmen and
assistants, came out in person to superintend the enterprise. He laid the foundations of a city to be
called Feliciana, near Fort San Carlos, and proceeded for some time with the work, when all his
enterprises were brought to a sudden termination by

the failure of his chief financial associate to supply him with the promised funds. M. Belly returned to France, where he has never since ceased to labor for the consummation of the schemes with which he had united his fortunes and his name so disastrously, and he made his appearance at the Paris Congress of 1879 as full of confidence and hope as ever.

Ten years afterward, the energetic assistance of the Emperor Napoleon, exasperated at the collapse of his plans in Mexico, enabled the illustrious economist and statesman, M. Michel Chevalier, to revive the French project of a Nicaraguan canal. M. Chevalier obtained, in conjunction with Don Tomas Ayon, of Nicaragua, a working contract for the construction of the canal, and arrangements were making at Paris to put the contract into execution, when they were suddenly suspended by the outbreak of the great Franco-German war. M. Chevalier has since died, but the imperial French tradition surviving him has been once more taken up, and with still greater energy, as we see, at the end of another decade, by Lieut. Bonaparte Wyse and the Viscount Ferdinand de Lesseps, who have simply changed the venue of the French schemes from Costa Rica and Nicaragua to the United States of Colombia.

This preliminary historical sketch is confined, it will be seen, chiefly to Nicaraguan projects, and this because these projects have chiefly engaged public attention during the last twenty years. More or less attention has always continued to be given, however, to the Tehuantepec, Panama, and Darien routes, all of which have at various times been strongly advocated. So far as our own country is concerned, the Nicaragua route has always been regarded with the most favor, both upon the ground of its practicability and for political reasons.

At the close of the civil war, the National Government again turned its attention to the interoceanic canal, as a subject which deserved immediate consideration. On the 19th of March, 1866, the Senate of the United States adopted the following resolution :

"*Resolved,* That the Secretary of the Navy furnish, through a report of the Superintendent of the Naval Observatory, the summit levels and distances by survey of the various proposed lines for interoceanic canals and railroads between the waters of the Atlantic and Pacific Oceans ; as, also their relative merits as practicable lines for the construction of a ship canal, and especially as relates to Honduras, Tehuantepec, Nicaragua, Panama, and Atrato lines; and also whether, in the opinion of the Superintendent, the Isthmus of Darien has been satisfactorily explored ; and if so, furnish in detail, charts, plans, lines of levels, and all information connected therewith, and upon what authority they are based."

In response to this resolution, Rear-Admiral Davis, on the 11th day of July, 1866, submitted a report containing a summary of the explorations and surveys which had been made prior to that time. This report, while making a clear presentation of the work which had already been done in the exploration of the isthmus, and incidentally illustrating the importance of an inter-oceanic canal, at the same time set forth the insufficiency of the data as yet obtained on the subject. Upon this point, Admiral Davis remarks:

"There does not exist in the libraries of the world the means of determining, even approximately, the most practicable route for a ship canal across the isthmus."

This report produced very important results; and the necessity was shown for further explorations and surveys, in order to determine the general feasibility of the work, and the selection of a route which, while presenting engineering difficulties capable of being overcome at the expense of a reasonable amount of capital, would serve sufficiently well the interests of commerce.

During the first term of President Grant's administration, the American government began a series of thorough and well-directed explorations, which have furnished more trustworthy information on this subject than had been obtained by the labors of all previous explorers during the preceding three hundred and fifty years.

It is unnecessary to examine the reports of these surveys in detail.   They embrace the surveys of the Tehuantepec route by Captain R.W. Shufeldt, of the Nicaragua route by Commander E. P. Lull and Civil Engineer A. G. Menocal, of the Atrato-Nipipi route by Lieutenant Collins and Commander Selfridge, and of the Panama route by the Navy Department. These surveys were all carefully and thoroughly examined by a commission appointed by President Grant, consisting of Brigadier-General Andrew A. Humphries, C. P. Patterson, Superintendent of the Coast Survey, and Rear-Admiral Ammen.

The result of the labors of this commission is stated in the report of the 7th of February, 1876, submitted to the President, from which we quote the following passage:

" *To the President of the United States:*

"The commission appointed by you to consider the subject of communication by canal between the waters of the Atlantic and Pacific Oceans, across, over, or near the isthmus connecting North and South America, have the honor, after a long, careful, and minute study of the several surveys of the various routes across the continent, unanimously to report:

"1. That the route known as the 'Nicaragua route,' beginning on the Atlantic side at or near Greytown; running by canal to the San Juan River, thence following its left bank to the mouth of the San Carlos River, at which point navigation of the San Juan River begins, and by the aid of three short canals of an aggregate length of 3·5 miles reaches Lake Nicaragua; from thence across the lake and through the valleys of the Rio del Medio and the Rio Grande, to what is known as the port of Brito, on the Pacific coast, possesses, both for the construction and maintenance of a canal, greater advantages, and offers fewer difficulties from engineering, commercial, and economic points of view, than any one of the other routes shown to be practicable by surveys sufficiently in detail to enable a judgment to be formed of their relative merits, as will be briefly presented in the appended memorandum."

The decision of this commission of experienced engineers must be accepted as entitled to great consideration with respect to the comparative merits of the several routes which were the subject of their examination. But the assumption, if advanced, that these are the only routes across the isthmus, is clearly untenable. The history of the subject shows that no thorough and exhaustive exploration from end to end of the mountain range which presents the barrier to the transit of the isthmus has yet been made.

Reports made from time to time by adventurous explorers warrant the opinion that this great engineering problem cannot be deemed to have received its final and complete solution until further scientific search has been made upon other lines of crossing than those so far examined.

A civil engineer, evidently of ability, in a recent letter to the *Alta* (San Francisco), *Californian,* makes the following suggestions toward further explorations:

"The solution of this question, 'Where can a practicable route for a ship canal through the Isthmus of Panama be found, upon which it can be built at a reasonable cost and in a few years of time?' is a question of orology, geology, topography, the chemistry of rocks and their relations, the metals in their relations to the mountain chains, and as the cause of local topography everywhere in metal-bearing countries, as is this isthmus region.

"The orologic system of the isthmus, from Porto Bello to Port David, on the Pacific, as shown by the maps and by all of the numerous surveys of that region, is this: That the course of all the mountains is about west north-west. Witness the San Blas Mountains, from Porto Bello to its junction with the Andes. Also, that the Panama Mountains follow the same course, and Selfridge's map, accompanying his report of 1871 or 1872, shows by the delineated river drainage that from Point Petillo, near Panama, eastward to the Andes, the mountain is missing— submerged.

"Now, mining experience declares that a low valley is all but universally, indeed we may with safety say *universally* and everywhere, found between the easterly and westerly chains, and hence a route will doubtless be found by ascending the Rio Juan de Dias to six to twelve miles north of Panama or thereabouts; a route through sedimentary rocks should be found at a low elevation, through to the Chagres and to the Atlantic.

"Southwest of Panama, a route should be looked for from Chami Bay through to the Rio Indios, on the Verajua shore, through a low east-and-west valley, between the Panama Mountains on the north and the Chami Mountains on the south.

"Another route, lying between the Chami Mountains on the north and the Chiriqui Mountains on the south, is to be looked for through the east-and-west valley extending from the Gulf of Parita, on the Pacific, through to the Rio Belem of Columbus.

"And a fourth route, which, if found, as I believe it can be, will probably be better than either of the others, is from Chiriqui Lagoon, in the Caribbean Sea, through to the Pacific, directly through the mountains to the east of the volcano of Chiriqui.

"Hitherto, exploration has been conducted to the

west of the volcano, but science points to that locality (east of the volcano) as the place to find an opening.

"Wheelwright, in his report upon this locality to the Royal Geographical Society, published by them in 1844, page 10, says, 'I was assured by several persons that a deep gorge had been discovered in the Untim Mountains,' etc., which seems to confirm this deduction.

"This Chiriqui Lagoon route has the farther advantages that it is outside of the one hundred mile limit, within which the Panama Railroad has control, viz., to secure certain defined pecuniary compensation, whereon a ship canal might be built. The distance between ports on the Atlantic and Pacific coasts of the United States is 150 miles shorter. It possesses unsurpassed harbors on both coasts, fine healthful climate, good soil, abundance of pure water, and coal in unlimited supply, for the steamers which must necessarily be employed in the carrying trade of the future."

That the canal problem should have been regarded as satisfactorily solved, rival routes determined upon, the requisite plans for the work elaborated, costly preparations made, and in more than one instance the undertaking actually begun, with the exploration of the isthmus as yet so incomplete is truly surprising.

The latest step of importance in the history of the projects for an American inter-oceanic canal is the call issued for a conference on the subject at Paris in May, 1879, under the nominal auspices of the Geographical Society of Paris ; in reality at the instance of the French company known as the "Commission Internationale d'Exploration." The professed object of this conference was the discussion of the best route for the inter-oceanic canal.

The American government *unofficially* authorized two eminent officers of the navy to attend the conference as delegates, in order that it might be informed of the results of the explorations made by the United States.

The true character of the Paris Conference of 1879 and the motives of its originators are described by the editor of the *North American Review* in an introductory note to an article by Mr. Menocal in the number of that periodical for September, 1879, as follows :

"It was rumored in Paris during the late Canal Congress, that the concession for the Darien canal, which was held by a little company of which General Türr is president, was divided into 100 shares of 500 francs each, and seemed to be understood that a company of 400,000,000 francs' capital would be formed to purchase the concession from the Türr company, and would pay the stockholders of this association 25,000,000 francs for their privileges. Thus each share of 500 francs would become worth 250,000 francs.

"With the fall of Sedan and the fortunes of the Second Empire, a large number of the most prominent Bonapartists lost their means of subsistence, and found themselves in a condition bordering on beggary. There were few men of private resources among them. Some had been placemen or stock speculators, while others had been the recipients of constant and liberal gifts from the emperor's privy purse. These gentlemen soon began to look to M. de Lesseps, a connection of the Empress Eugenie, for help and guidance. He alone, of this helpless and hungry crowd, could command the credit and confidence of capitalists. To pierce the isthmus of Central America had been the cherished wish of Louis Napoleon, and this project was not long in recurring to his dejected followers. Thus the scheme was revived and matured under the sponsorship and direction of M. de Lesseps, the executive duties of the undertaking devolving upon Lieutenant Bonaparte Wyse, whose sister is married to General Türr.

"A careful examination of the names of the French delegates to the Canal Congress shows how entirely it was packed with subservient friends of the fallen dynasty; nor is it well to overlook the fact that the shares of the Türr Company were largely held by them. These people once went to Mexico to seek their fortunes in a Franco-Mexican Empire. It seems passing strange that the conspicuous defeat of those plans, which embraced the destruction of the American Union, should have failed to teach them some degree of caution before affecting to despise the views of the American envoys from Washington, or attempting to tamper with American interests in America."

Comment upon the motives which inspired the proceedings of the convention is foreign to the purpose of this paper, except with respect to their political significance. In this aspect, however, the scheme which received the sanction of this convention demands the grave consideration of the American people. It is plain that the originators of the Wyse-Lesseps canal project rely largely for the success of the enterprise upon the belief that it will, when completed, extend the power and influence of the Latin race in general, and promote the interests of France in particular. The failure of France to maintain a footing in Mexico is to be compensated for by the construction of an inter-oceanic canal upon neighboring territory and under French auspices. French capital is to levy tribute upon the commerce of the globe, establishing upon the American Isthmus a Latin stronghold, to the effectual obstruction of the extension of Anglo-Saxon dominion and influence.

That M. de Lesseps can count upon the cordial support not only of his own government, but also of other European powers, can be doubted by no one familiar with European policy where European interests are involved. A failure to see the main chance and to grasp it, is *not* among the defects of monarchical institutions.

THE authorship and origin of the Monroe doctrine have at various times been subjects of discussion. Sumner says that Canning was its inventor,
promoter, and champion, and the same claim sub-
stantially has been made on behalf of Jefferson,
John Quincy Adams, and Monroe. It is unquestionably true that the suggestions made in the sum-
mer of 1823, by Canning to Mr. Rush, then American Minister at London, when reported by him to
the Department of State at Washington, were the
means of calling the attention of Mr. Monroe and
his cabinet to the subject. One of the questions
which Mr. Canning asked Mr. Rush was, "Were the
great political and commercial interests, which hung
upon the destinies of the new continent, to be can-
vassed and adjusted in Europe without the co-operation, or even the knowledge of the United States?"

This question of Canning's contains the germ of
the Monroe doctrine. When Mr. Rush's dispatches

on the subject were received at Washington, the President sent copies to Jefferson and Madison, and consulted them on the subject. They both favored the policy of acting in conjunction with England in opposition to the designs of the Holy Alliance of interfering in this hemisphere to restore to Spain her revolted colonies. When the matter of determining what political form the action of our country should take came up, it was Mr. Adams's business, as the member of the cabinet who had charge of the management of our foreign affairs, to determine upon what principles our official declarations on the subject should be founded. Mr. Calhoun, who was also a member of Monroe's cabinet, says that Adams was the author of the declarations which are now known as those of the President who indorsed them. Mr. Calhoun is sustained by the fact that in those days, as is now the case, the Secretary of State was accustomed to write the portions of the messages relative to foreign affairs, and in this case the draft made by Mr. Adams in that capacity was adopted without change.

THE attempts to carry into effect the Lesseps-Wyse scheme for constructing an inter-oceanic canal under French auspices, bring the question home to Americans, and make it necessary for us to consider practically whether that scheme can be carried out consistently with the Monroe doctrine, which, as laid down in President Monroe's annual message of December 2d, 1823, consists of two propositions:

First. In speaking of the controversy as to the North-western boundary, and the proposed arrangements with Great Britain and Russia, the message uses the following language:

"In the discussions to which this interest has given rise, and in the arrangements in which they may terminate, the occasion has been judged proper for asserting as a *principle* in which the rights and interests of the United States are involved, that the American continents, by the free and independent

43

condition which they have assumed and maintained, are henceforth not to be considered as subjects for future colonization by any European power."

In order to properly interpret this passage, the political condition of the continents referred to at the time it was written must be considered. There did not then exist upon either of them any territory outside of the limits of the United States which was not claimed by some European power. The protest was directed against the occupation of any territory upon either continent, upon the pretense that it was unoccupied, and this without any reference to whether the territory involved was or was not claimed by the United States. Mr. Monroe spoke not for his own country merely, nor even chiefly; but for every other American republic. He asserted an abstract principle. It was a broad declaration to the effect that territorial questions touching these continents were henceforth to be managed by the "free and independent" states already established upon them. It was the announcement of a principle of foreign policy of peculiar significance, and it should be recognized as a permanent and controlling tenet governing our relations with foreign powers. It means that no European power can be permitted to gain a foothold upon the American continents, either by direct colonization, political intrigue, or the not less dangerous agency of gigantic foreign

corporations, more powerful than the states upon
whose territory they are fixed.

Second. In another part of the same message, Mr.
Monroe, in speaking of the condition of the people
of Spain and Portugal, and of their efforts to im-
prove their condition, efforts frustrated by the interference of the Holy Alliance, says:

"In the wars of the European powers, in matters
relating to themselves, we have never taken any
part, nor does it comport with our policy so to do.
It is only when our rights are invaded or seriously
menaced, that we resent injuries, or make preparations for our defense. With the movements in this
hemisphere we are of necessity more immediately
connected, and by causes which must be obvious to
all enlightened and impartial observers. The political system of the allied powers is essentially different in this respect from that of America. This
difference proceeds from that which exists in their
respective governments. And to the defense of our
own, which has been achieved by the loss of so
much blood and treasure, and matured by the wisdom of our most enlightened citizens, and under
which we have enjoyed an unexampled felicity, the
whole nation is devoted. We owe it, therefore, to
candor and to the amicable relations existing between the United States and those powers to declare,
that we should consider any attempt on their part to

extend their system to any portion of this hemisphere as dangerous to our peace and safety. With existing colonies or dependencies of any European power we have not interfered, and shall not interfere. But with the governments who have declared their independence and maintained it, and whose independence we have, on great considerations and on just principles, acknowledged, we could not view any interposition, for the purpose of oppressing them, or controlling in any other manner their destiny, by any European power, in any other light than as the manifestation of an unfriendly disposition toward the United States. In the war between those new governments and Spain, we declared our neutrality at the time of their recognition; and to this we have adhered, and we shall continue to adhere, provided no change shall occur which, in the judgment of the competent authorities of this government, shall make a corresponding change on the part of the United States indispensable to their security."

Speaking of the intervention of the Holy Alliance in the internal affairs of Spain, Mr. Monroe says:

"To what extent such interposition may be carried, on the same principle, is a question in which all independent powers whose governments differ from theirs are interested, and even those most remote, and surely none more so than the United States.

"Our policy in regard to Europe, which was adopted at an early stage of the wars which have so long agitated that quarter of the globe, nevertheless remains the same; which is, not to interfere in the internal concerns of any of its powers; to consider the government *de facto* as the legitimate government for us; to cultivate friendly relations with it; and to preserve these relations by a frank, firm, and manly policy, meeting in all instances the just claims of every power, submitting to injuries from none. But, in regard to these continents, circumstances are eminently and conspicuously different. It is impossible that the allied powers should extend this political system to any portion of either continent without endangering our peace and happiness; nor can we believe that our Southern brethren, if left to themselves, would adopt it of their own accord. It is equally impossible, therefore, that we should behold such interposition in any form with indifference. If we look to the comparative strength and resources of Spain and these new governments, and their distance from each other, it must be obvious that she can never subdue them. It is still the true policy of the United States to leave the parties to themselves, in the hope that other powers will pursue the same course."

In this portion of the message, the non-intervention policy laid down in Washington's Farewell Address is reaffirmed so far as the affairs of Europe are concerned, but it is distinctly asserted that as to this hemisphere that policy does not apply.

The message contemplates positive and affirmative resistance to any action tending to give European powers any increase of territory or of influence in the New World. The language used with reference to this subject is very comprehensive. It declares that we must consider any attempt upon the part of European powers to extend their system to any part of this hemisphere, as "dangerous to our peace and safety." But it does not stop there. It declares that this government cannot permit any interference of the powers of Europe for the purpose of oppressing any of the states of these continents, "*or controlling in any other manner their destiny.*" Plainly the language of this message meant that we thereby assumed the protectorate of the republics upon the Western continents. It emphatically prohibits any interference by European powers calculated to control their destiny in any manner whatever. It means that American affairs must be controlled by Americans, and that we, as the leading American power, *will* see to the enforcement of this doctrine.

It has been alleged, even in this country, that the Monroe doctrine never had any binding force. In a discussion which arose in 1855–1856 in relation to its applicability to Central American affairs, particular efforts were made, chiefly by Whig statesmen and writers, to limit its extent. One writer, in particular, in the *North American Review*, argued that this doctrine was practically nothing more than a *brutum fulmen*, that it "was intended to meet a particular contingency of events, and therefore passed away with the occasion which called it forth." It is true that this doctrine has never received by formal declaration the express sanction of the legislative branch of the government. As Mr. Seward well observed, in the debate upon the subject in the United States Senate, in 1855, this was largely owing to the fact that it is an abstract principle, with respect to which no occasion of practical exigency had then arisen calling for Congressional legislation.

The mere fact, however, that the Monroe doctrine has never received the formal indorsement of Congress, has neither diminished its moral effect, nor impaired its practical efficacy whenever the opportunity for its assertion has occurred.

The French invasion of Mexico presented a conspicuous instance of its application. The presence of General Sheridan on our south-western frontier, with seventy thousand men, a part of the great army placed in the field by the order of Congress for the national defense, effectually dispensed with

4

the necessity of specific legislation to secure the withdrawal of the French forces.

The Monroe doctrine, in short, is simply the extension to all the political communities of the New World of the declaration made by our ancestors for the British colonies in 1776, that they were, "and of right ought to be free and independent states." Hence its firm and profound hold on the popular heart and will of this country.

The vast moral influence resulting from the mere enunciation of principles of public policy by the American Executive, is well illustrated by the extent to which Washington's Farewell Address has shaped the foreign and domestic policy of this republic. In very many important particulars that document has been as efficacious as if it had been embodied in our statutes.

It would be absurd to argue that that paper is entitled to no consideration, because it was never formally approved by a resolution of Congress. Such, however, is the only objection of any real weight which has ever been made against the Monroe doctrine.

In order to understand the full weight and import of this principle, it is proper to refer to the manner in which it was received in Europe at the time it was promulgated. Never did any American state paper, except the Declaration of Independence, excite greater interest there. "It was," says Sumner, "upon all tongues; the press was full of it; the securities of Spanish America rose in the market; the agents of Spanish America were happy." Mr. Brougham said in his place in Parliament, "An event has recently happened than which none has ever dispersed greater joy, exultation, and gratitude over all the free men of Europe; that event, which is decisive on the subject, is the language held with respect to Spanish America in the message of the President of the United States."

Sir James Mackintosh seems to have understood the full scope and true meaning of the language used by President Monroe. Speaking in reference to it, he said: "That wise government, in grave but determined language, and with the reasonable but deliberate tone that becomes true courage, proclaims the principles of her policy, and makes known the cases in which the care of her own safety will compel her to take up arms for the defense of other States. I have already observed its coincidence with the declarations of England, which indeed is perfect, if allowance be made for the deeper, or at least more immediate interest in the independence of South America which near neighborhood gives the United States. This coincidence of the two great English commonwealths (for so I delight to call them, and I heartily pray that they may be forever united in the cause of justice and liberty) cannot be contemplated without the utmost pleasure by every enlightened citizen of the earth."

The boldness of President Monroe in assuming the ground he did was worthy of all admiration. Well-founded rumors were then current as to the designs of the great powers of continental Europe. The brief reports of the discussions of the subject in Mr. Monroe's cabinet, which have come down to us, show that this government had grave fears of European intervention in American affairs in a manner exceedingly dangerous to our national safety. Thus John Quincy Adams in his diary mentions as among the probable schemes of the Holy Alliance, the seizure of California, Peru, and Chili, by Russia; of Mexico by France, and of Cuba by England. It was thought to be well established that France had been intriguing for the establishment of monarchies in Mexico, and in Buenos Ayres, under princes of the house of Bourbon.

Mr. Adams had apparently very full and trustworthy information as to certain designs of the great powers threatening to our country. Thus he learned from a letter from Mr. Gallatin that the French Minister of Foreign Affairs, M. Hyde de Neuville, had said to him in the hearing of ten or twelve persons that if we did not yield to the claim of France under the eighth article of the Louisiana Convention, she ought to go and take the country back, and that she had a strong party there. Such things show the gravity of the situation at that time and the dangers then at our own doors.

The apprehensions of our statesmen were not limited to the prospects of foreign intervention alone. They included also the perils of European colonization upon the American continents. And this constitutes the other branch of this subject as it is treated in the celebrated message of President Monroe. Mr. Webster thus forcibly states the foundation upon which this principle of the Monroe doctrine rests :

"Great and practical inconveniences it was feared might be apprehended from the establishment of new colonies in America, having a European origin and a European connection. Attempts of that kind, it was obvious, might possibly be made amidst the changes that were taking place in Mexico, *as well as in the more southern states.* Mexico bounds us on a vast line from the Gulf of Mexico to the Pacific Ocean. There are many reasons why it is not to be desired by us that an establishment under the protection of a different power *should occupy any portion of that space.*"

There is abundant contemporary testimony to the enthusiasm with which the announcement of the Monroe doctrine was received among our people.

They felt its evident and lasting applicability to
American affairs ; and that this profound conviction
of our people was not a mere evanescent feeling, born
of the circumstances of the hour, is shown by the
unanimity with which the reassertion of the principle is now demanded throughout the length and
breadth of the land.   To this manly declaration of
rights Americans of all shades of political opinion
have always subscribed.   In the debate on the Panama mission, in the House of Representatives, Mr.
Webster, in speaking of the popular approbation of
the Monroe doctrine, said :

"It met with the entire concurrence and the hearty
approbation of the country.   The tone in which it
was uttered found a corresponding response in the
breasts of the free people of the United States.   The
people saw, and they rejoiced to see, that, on a fit occasion, our weight had been thrown into the right
scale, and that, without departing from our duty, we
had done something useful and something effectual
for the cause of civil liberty.

"One general glow of exultation, one universal
feeling of the gratified love of liberty, one conscious
and proud perception of the consideration which the
country possessed, and of the respect and honor
which belonged to it, pervades all her sons."

John Quincy Adams, who at least assisted at the
council board at which the doctrine was originally

considered and put into shape, if he did not himself formulate it, by no means understood it to be limited to the condition of affairs which existed in 1823. Writing to Mr. Gallatin on the 20th of March, 1827, Mr. Adams remarks :

"As the assertion of this principle is an attitude which the American hemisphere must assume, *it is one which no European has the right to question;* and if the inference drawn from it of danger to existing colonies has any foundation, it can only be on the contingency of a war, which we shall by all means avoid."

Mr. Jefferson, on the 24th of October, 1823, wrote to Mr. Monroe :

" Our first and fundamental maxim should be, never to entangle ourselves in the broils of Europe ; our second, never to suffer Europe to meddle with cis-atlantic affairs." He thus goes even further than Mr. Monroe in his opposition to European interference in American concerns. In the same letter, speaking of the proposed policy, he says :

"Its object is to introduce and establish the American system of keeping out of our land all foreign powers, or never permitting those of Europe to intermeddle with the affairs of our nations. It is to maintain our own principle, not to depart from it."

These views contemplate the exercise of a practical protectorate over all the Spanish-American States.

Mr. Jefferson argues in decided opposition to "the transfer to any power by conquest, cession, or *acquisition in any other way, of any of* the Spanish-American States."

Mr. Webster regarded the message of 1823 not only as of vast importance to the nation, but also as embodying principles of public policy of permanent applicability. In a speech in Congress on this subject, he said :

"The country has, in my judgment, a very high honor connected with that occurrence, which we may maintain or which we may sacrifice. I look upon it as part of its treasures of reputation, and, for one, I intend to guard it. . . . . Sir, I look on the message of December, 1823, as forming a bright page in our history. I will help neither to erase it nor to tear it out ; nor shall it be, by any act of mine, blurred or blotted. It did honor to the sagacity of the government, and I will not diminish that honor. It elevated the hopes and gratified the patriotism of the people. Over those hopes I will not bring a mildew, nor will I put that gratified patriotism to shame."

Mr. W. H. Trescot, whose contributions to the history of American diplomacy constitute so valuable a part of the literature of our country, refers to the Monroe doctrine in terms which indicate that he regards it not as a mere expression of opinion upon a temporary occasion, but as the promulgation of a principle for our enduring guidance in our national foreign policy. In his history of the diplomacy of the administrations of Washington and Adams, he says, speaking of the first generation of statesmen produced by our country :

"With rare courage and temper and wisdom, they had laid broad the foundations of a great country, and with singular good fortune, had been permitted to perfect the government which they had initiated. For more than a quarter of a century, the men who framed the Constitution were allowed to administer it ; and having thus formed it in infancy, and moulded its youth, they retired one after another from the scenes of their great achievements, leaving to a new generation the responsibility of its mature manhood. But, as if to consecrate with the grace of their final benediction its foremost step, it was granted to Mr. Monroe, the last of the venerable company, to *inaugurate, by his famous declaration, the vigorous commencement of our national life.* From the date of that declaration, our foreign policy, if it has not taken a higher tone, has at least expressed itself in a more systematic development."

It may, however, well be questioned whether the interests of the present administration, under the peculiar circumstances of an existing emergency calling for the most energetic expression of our traditional policy, is not open to just criticism. Making every allowance for the fact that the inception of action of the character suggested is ordinarily secret, and that the administration has appreciated and is preparing to act upon the emergency, yet it is no less true that several months have passed away since the necessity for action became manifest, and preparation has not culminated in fruition.

There are requirements of national importance which do not admit of an hour's delay. This is one of them. Affairs have advanced during the last six months on the Isthmus of Darien to a stage where negotiation and diplomacy are wholly inappropriate and cannot possibly avail. While the necessity has always existed for our control of the thoroughfare to our western coasts, events have now made that necessity instant and imperious. It can be trifled with no longer.

The Monroe doctrine was reaffirmed by Mr. Polk in his message to Congress of December 2d, 1845. He says:

"In the existing circumstances of the world the present is deemed a proper occasion to reiterate and reaffirm the principle avowed by Mr. Monroe, and to state my cordial concurrence in its wisdom and sound policy. Existing rights of every nation should be respected; but it is due alike to our safety and our interests that the efficient protection of our laws should be extended over our whole territorial limits; and it should be distinctly announced to the world as our settled policy, that no future European colony or dominion shall, with our consent, be planted or established on any part of the North American continent."

A great canal corporation, controlled in Europe, and under European laws, would inevitably exercise dominion in Central America, if established there.

Mr. Cass, a statesman whose accurate and extensive knowledge of the history and spirit of the foreign policy of this country should entitle his opinions to great weight, in a debate in the Senate of the United States on the 28th of January, 1856, used the following language in regard to the extent and applicability of the Monroe doctrine:

"It is inexplicable, sir, that any one could suppose that these declarations had reference only to the peculiar position of the Spanish colonies. The first had, but the second was addressed to all nations, *and was intended to operate during all time.* It was the annunciation of a new line of policy. On what was it founded? On the situation of our country, and of the various states of this continent, which demanded a system, as Mr. Jefferson said, 'separate and apart from that of Europe.'"

Mr. Buchanan, in his "History of the Origin and Nature of the Monroe Doctrine," says:

"It soon became a canon of faith for the American people, and they placed it side by side with their hostility to the imprisonment of American seamen, and to the search of American vessels on the high seas."

Although the doctrine in question is hostile to the extension of European influence upon this continent, it has been constantly recognized by European writers as a weighty protest against all interference by foreign powers upon the American continent.

Sir Edward Creasy, in his work on "International Law," while denying the validity of the Monroe doctrine, admits that there are strong proofs of its prevalence in the United States, and that the United States "has at times assumed the position of the exclusively leading power of the New World."

Commander Pim, R. N., in his "Gate of the Pacific," refers to the doctrine as designed to secure for the United States "the sole and exclusive right to the commerce of the New World." This writer perhaps gives us credit for more sagacity in our foreign policy than we are entitled to. The wisdom of our people has not been conspicuously shown of late years in the development of American commerce.

A writer in the London *Quarterly Review* for January, 1862, said, "President Pierce, when he came into office, avowed his adherence to what is called the Monroe doctrine, which in effect amounts to this,—that no European power has the right to interfere with any part of the continent of America south of the frontier of Canada. Indeed, we are not sure that it even excludes Canada."

In the same year, a writer in the London *Times*, referring to the French invasion of Mexico, said:

"It would be vain to deny that the feeling of the merchants of London is, that on the whole, so far as the affair has proceeded, the Emperor Napoleon has done a great service, both politically and commercially, to the world; politically in confirming the previous action of Spain in *extinguishing the Monroe doctrine*, and commercially in restoring the intercourse of nations with a territory, which, from its geographical position and mineral wealth, can claim a general and almost exceptional importance."

If we turn to the diplomatic history of the United States, we find the Monroe doctrine unequivocally recognized in the instructions issued to the ministers of the United States whenever the occasion demanded.

Mr. Clay, as Secretary of State under Mr. Adams, in his instructions to Mr. Poinsett, the delegate to the Panama Congress, dated May 25, 1825, used the following language with reference to one branch of the Monroe doctrine:

"The countries in which any such new establishments might be attempted are now open to the enterprise and commerce of all Americans, and the justice and propriety cannot be recognized of arbitrarily limiting and circumscribing that enterprise and commerce by the act of voluntarily planting a new colony, without the consent of America, under the auspices of foreign powers belonging to another and a distant continent. Europe would be indignant at an attempt to plant a colony on any part of her shores; and her justice must perceive, in the rule contended for, only perfect reciprocity."

Mr. Cass, when Secretary of State under Mr. Buchanan, instructed Mr. Lamar, our minister at that time to Central America, in the following terms, with reference to this subject :

"But the establishment of a political protectorate by any one of the powers of Europe over any of the independent states of this continent, or, in other words, *the introduction of a scheme of policy which would carry with it a right to interfere in their concerns*, is a measure to which the United States have long since avowed their opposition, and which, should the attempt be made, they will resist by all the means in their power.

"The reasons for the attitude they have assumed have been promulgated, and are everywhere well known. There is no need upon this occasion to recapitulate them. They are founded upon the political circumstances of the American continent, which has interests of its own, and ought to have a policy of its own disconnected from many of the questions which are continually presenting themselves in Europe concerning the balance of power, and other subjects of controversy arising out of the condition of its states, and which often find their solution or their postponement in war."

On the 31st of December, 1855, Mr. Cass said in the Senate, that he had always been in favor of asserting and maintaining the Monroe doctrine, and that Congress had never indorsed it only because it was thought unnecessary to assert an abstraction. He furthermore said on the same occasion, that it was our duty to maintain "the continental rights of our position."

The joint proposition, in 1852, of Great Britain and France to enter into a tripartite convention with the United States to guarantee in perpetuity to Spain the possession of Cuba, afforded Mr. Everett, then Secretary of State, an opportunity to assert the principles of the Monroe doctrine, of which he promptly availed himself.

His language is guarded and moderate, but none the less forcible on that account. He says, in declining to enter into the proposed convention, that it "would be of no value unless it were lasting; accordingly its terms express a perpetuity of purpose and obligation."

Mr. Everett then expresses doubts as to whether it would be competent for the treaty-making powers to enter into such an agreement. Referring to the fact that in 1803 the United States purchased Louisiana of France, and in 1819 Florida of Spain, he observes that—

"The United States would, by the proposed convention, disable themselves from making an acquisition which might take place without any disturbance of existing foreign relations, and in the natural order of things;" and, calling attention to the great law of American growth and progress, to the protection of which the Monroe doctrine is so essential, he adds:

"It would seem impossible for any one who reflects upon the events glanced at in this note, to mistake the law of American growth and progress, or think that it can ultimately be arrested by a convention like that proposed. In the judgment of the President, it would be as easy to throw a dam from Cape Florida to Cuba to stop the flow of the Gulf Stream, as to attempt by a compact like this to fix the fortunes of Cuba for all coming time."

The prophetic language of the Abbé Grègoire, writing in Paris in 1808, anticipates these views. "The American Continent, asylum of liberty," he writes, "is moving toward an order of things which *will be common to the Antilles, and the course of which all the powers combined cannot arrest."*

M. Michel Chevalier, who contracted in 1868, as we have shown, with Nicaragua, for the construction of a French ship canal, urges in his work on Mexico, published in 1864, the importance of the establishment of the empire of Maximilian as a means of effectually correcting the "American view of the force of the Monroe doctrine." And Sir Edward Creasy, already referred to, says, in speaking of the French occupation of Mexico :

"The United States (occupied by their own civil war, which was then raging) did not actually send troops to oppose the French in Mexico, but they steadily refused to recognize Maximilian, or any government, except a republican government, in Mexico ; and the language of their statesmen exhibited the fullest development of the Monroe doctrine. In a circular addressed by the American minister, Mr. Seward, to the legations of the United States, he said that 'In the President's judgment the emancipation of the American continent from the control of Europe has been the principal feature of the last half century.'

"In April, 1864, the Chamber of Representatives at Washington voted unanimously a declaration that 'It is not fitting for the people of the United States to recognize a monarchical government erected

5

on the ruins of a republican government in America under the auspices of any European power whatever.' "

That the incorporation by Great Britain, in 1867, of all her North American possessions as one great province—the Dominion of Canada—was clearly in derogation of the spirit of the Monroe doctrine, must be conceded. The establishment of the Dominion of Canada was intended to strengthen the hold of a European power upon territory so situated geographically that its acquisition by this country has been regarded by eminent British statesmen as only a question of time. The event did not pass unnoticed in this country, but was the occasion of an extreme and pointed indorsement of the Monroe doctrine by the popular branch of Congress.

A resolution was unanimously adopted by the House of Representatives, declaring the uneasiness of the United States in the contemplation of " such a vast conglomeration of American states established on the monarchical principle—such a proceeding being in contravention of the *traditionary and constantly declared principles* of the United States, and endangering their most important interest."

Mr. Seward, in 1856, predicted that Canada would belong to us within fifty years ; and in making the subsequent acquisition of Alaska, this far-seeing statesman, then Secretary of State, looked forward to the consummation of a plan of territorial acquisition which embraced the continent.

No ! the message of December 3, 1823, was by no means a mere high-sounding state paper ! It put an end to projects very dangerous to the safety of the United States. It created in America a lasting sentiment of opposition to foreign intrusion upon the affairs of the western continents. It made emphatic proclamation to Europe that she would never more be permitted to aggrandize herself at the expense of this hemisphere. The grave consequences which followed the simple promulgation of our foreign policy, as outlined by the declaration of President Monroe, were not the empty reverberations of a *brutum fulmen.* In the language of Mr. Cass:

"This great cis-atlantic principle does not derive its strength from its origin, or its author; it rests upon a surer foundation, upon the cordial concurrence of the American people, and is destined to be a broad line upon the chart of their policy."

THE foreign policy of the United States was in its earliest stages largely shaped by the dread of foreign interference.

A conservative and neutral policy was undoubtedly the part of wisdom. There were, however, many influences which tended to draw us into dangerous foreign connections. There was a party in the country which, at the close of the war of independence, sought the establishment of a monarchy under the sovereignty of Washington, and plans were afoot for offering the crown to Prince Henry of Prussia, even after the adoption of the Constitution of 1789.

The wealth and intelligence of its members gave this faction greater strength than its mere numerical numbers indicated, and it was long feared that it might invite foreign interference for the accomplishment of its purpose.

68

The weakness of the executive branch of the national government, not only under the Confederation but even under the Constitution, with respect to the administration of foreign affairs, was peculiarly felt. The power of declaring war was vested in Congress alone, and the treaty-making power in the President and Senate jointly ; and the government found it difficult to act in the conduct of its foreign affairs with the promptness and vigor of powers whose executives were not so restricted. The inconveniences of these constitutional provisions are now less felt than at a time when the open hostility and secret intrigues of foreign powers were a source of constant apprehension to us.

Our weakness in this respect was made evident during the commotions produced by the French Revolution, and especially during the difficulties which grew out of the war between England and France. The condition of our country at that period is graphically described by Wharton :

"To draw the American people from their neutrality, first by coaxing, then by bullying, had been the object of each of the belligerent powers. Provocations to war, as well as solicitations for alliance, had been given on both sides, and as alliance with both, or war with both seemed impracticable, the question was which to choose. Of all questions by which a country can be agitated, that as to which

of two foreign alliances is to be accepted is the
most demoralizing; and to the worst type of this
dangerous disease the temperament of the American
people rendered them susceptible." *

The efforts of French emissaries to force upon us
an alliance with France form a familiar and humil-
iating chapter in the history of the country.

M. Genet, the first minister of the French Republic to the United States, on landing at Charleston,
S. C., in April, 1793, forthwith opened a correspondence with American citizens, urging a determined
opposition to the policy of Washington's administration. This purpose he vigorously pursued in the
face of the proclamation of neutrality, and by direct
appeals to the passions of the populace; privateers
were fitted out at Charleston, to cruise against vessels of nations at peace with the United States; hostile expeditions were projected against Florida and
Louisiana, the provinces of Spain. Insulting and
domineering as was the course pursued by Genet, a
large party in the country was actually willing to
see the nation thus humiliated to promote the interests of a foreign power.

On the other hand, there was a party scarcely less
submissive to English interests. It was composed
chiefly of those whose latent loyalty to England had
survived the war which separated the colonies from

* Wharton's American State Trials, p. 7.

the mother country, and who had never lost their fondness for the land which in childhood they had been taught to regard as their home. These rival foreign attachments produced very disastrous consequences. To use the language of a foreigner, quoted by Tucker in his "Life of Jefferson," "the year 1800 found many French and many English, but few Americans." *

So utterly wanting in national pride and spirit were our countrymen thought to be, that in 1791 the Spanish governor of New Orleans made a proposition to Judge Innis, a leading citizen of Ohio, looking to the secession of the western territory from the Union, the inducement to this step being the free navigation of the Mississippi.

Under such circumstances the Farewell Address of Washington was issued, and the foreign policy of the United States dates from its promulgation. Its wisdom and its applicability to the internal condition and foreign relations of the country, at the time, justifies the following extract from its statesmanlike and philosophical expositions of our duty as a people.

"A passionate attachment of one nation for another produces a variety of evils. Sympathy for the favorite nation, facilitating the illusion of an imaginary common interest in cases where no real com-

* 2 Tucker's Life of Jefferson, p. 19.

mon interest exists, and infusing into one the enmities of the other, betrays the former into a participation in the quarrels and wars of the latter, without adequate inducement or justification. . . . It gives to ambitious, corrupted, or deluded citizens, who devote themselves to the favorite nation, facility to betray or sacrifice the interests of their own country, without odium, sometimes even with popularity. . . .

"An attachment of a small or weak toward a great and powerful nation, dooms the former to be the satellite of the latter."

It was the language of devoted and exalted patriotism addressed to a people whose zealous party complications in the strife of France and England had suppressed, almost destroyed, the sentiment of attachment to their own country. Equally applicable to the relations then existing between the United States and European powers are these words, in which the elementary principles of our foreign policy are declared:

"Europe has a set of primary interests, which to us have no or a very remote relation. . . . Hence, therefore, it must be unwise for us to implicate ourselves by artificial ties in the ordinary vicissitudes of her politics, or the ordinary combinations of her friendships or enmities. . . . Why quit our own to stand upon foreign ground? . . .

Against the insidious wiles of foreign influence . . . the jealousy of a free people ought to be constantly awake. . . ."

Such language, however, addressed to a people engrossed in the consideration of exciting domestic questions, was an argument against the adoption of a policy looking to the increase of the power and influence of the nation by prudent and well-considered diplomatic measures. Sound as are the doctrines laid down, a strict adherence to the letter rather than the spirit of the advice has unquestionably done much to render our foreign policy halting and timid, and whenever questions affecting our external relations have arisen, the influence of the strict construction of the language of the Farewell Address has been felt. When the question of the indorsement of the Monroe doctrine was under consideration in Congress, in 1856, Mr. Cass, with his usual astuteness, pointed to the real considerations which restrained our statesmen from the formal sanction of a declaration so necessary to the protection of our national interests. "It was," said Mr. Cass, "some undefined apprehension that if we spoke the words we must adhere to them, and that if we adhered to them they would be words of terrible import to our country."

As is well observed by Mr. Trescot, the chief feature of the foreign policy of the United States, dur-

ing the early history of the nation, was its negative character ; its aim was to prevent rather than to
accomplish. The truth of this assertion is well illustrated by the history of our diplomacy during the
European wars which followed the French Revolution. The hesitating and inconsistent spirit of our
diplomacy may be illustrated by leading incidents
throughout its entire history.

1. In May, 1818, an accredited emissary from the
Ionian Islands called upon Mr. Rush, then the
American Minister at the Court of St. James, to ask
if the Constitution of the United States prohibited
the acquisition of foreign territory. Mr. Rush replied in the negative. He was asked if it would
accord with our policy to assume a protectorate
over the Ionian Islands, and informed that such a
protectorate would be promptly accepted.   Mr.
Rush summarily declined to consider the proposition, on the ground that its acceptance would involve
our entrance upon the arena of European politics.
This was a reply strictly in accordance with our true
policy of non-interference.

A refusal, in 1823, to accept the proffered annexation of Central America, rests on wholly different
grounds, and is an instance of the singular timidity
of our foreign policy.   It is thus referred to by Mr.
Everett :

"When this interesting region, a country more

than twice as large as Great Britain, and possessing resources not inferior to any country in the world, declared its independence of Spain, and formed, with its five infant republics, a federal government, it resolved, by the unanimous vote of its representatives to seek admission into the American Union, and sent an embassy of eight of its most respectable citizens to Washington to effect that object." This was a case for interference. Had this offer been accepted, it would have solved, once for all, the problem of the control of the inter-oceanic canal.

It would have placed the United States in that commanding position in regard to the commerce of the world to which the sagacity of Patterson, one hundred and twenty years before, had pointed, and given us control of what he aptly described as the "door of the seas."

The treaty by which Louisiana was acquired in 1803 forms a notable exception to the general timid conservatism which characterized the conduct of our diplomacy during its early history, and by establishing the constitutional power of the national government to acquire foreign territory, it gave a wider scope to the exercise of American diplomacy and statesmanship, and set up a standing precedent for judicious territorial expansion.

The Louisiana precedent was followed in 1819 by

the treaty with Spain for the cession of Florida to the United States.

That transaction, although not very creditable to the statesmanship of Monroe and his cabinet, cannot upon the whole be condemned as unwise or inexpedient. The measure was severely criticised at the time in Congress, by Mr. Clay, who said we had bought for a high price a possession which must inevitably have fallen into our lap, and that nothing would have been lost by waiting a little longer. He called attention to the fact that, under the articles by which the boundaries were fixed between Louisiana and Mexico, Texas had been sacrificed in addition to the $30,000,000 needlessly, as he claimed, paid for Florida. In the same debate, Mr. Clay raised the question as to the constitutional power of the treaty-making branch of the government to cede territory belonging to the nation. In the same connection, referring to the proposition which had been made by Russia to mediate in the settlement of our troubles with Spain, Mr. Clay used the following language in relation to the position we ought to assume with reference to foreign powers :

"It was to invite further interposition. It might in the process of time create in the bosom of our country a Russian faction, a British faction, a French faction. Every nation ought to be jealous of this species of interference, whatever was its form of government. But of all forms of government, the united testimony of all history admonished a republic to be most guarded against it. From the moment Philip intermeddled with the affairs of Greece, the liberty of Greece was doomed to inevitable destruction."

Great as was the influence which Thomas Jefferson had in moulding our political institutions, and in determining the spirit of their administration, he was equally influential in shaping for many years our foreign policy. The weight of his administrative authority, except in the case of Louisiana, was thrown in favor of a cautious and timorous course with reference to all external relations of the country.

The following paragraph from his notes on Virginia seems to contain the principle upon which he both advised and conducted the administration of our foreign affairs.

"You ask me," he writes, "what I think of the expediency of encouraging our States to become commercial. Were I to indulge my own theory, I wish them to practice neither commerce nor navigation ; but to stand with regard to Europe precisely on the footing of China."

This surprising doctrine of foreign policy was no mere theory with Jefferson, but was by him and his personal followers carried into practice. They refused to strengthen the navy, and failed to place the army upon the footing dictated by the commonest prudence in the then condition of the country. The disastrous embargo was its direct and immediate consequence—a measure which illustrates how little the statesmen of that day knew of the proper management of our relations with foreign powers. The time came when Jefferson himself, repenting of this undignified and unpatriotic policy, became a staunch champion of the Monroe doctrine.

The nominal object of the embargo was to force England and France to revoke the orders in council and the Berlin and Milan decrees. It utterly failed to accomplish the purpose intended. It greatly benefited England. It excited no gratitude on the part of France. It swept from the ocean ten thousand American vessels engaged in a profitable carrying trade, and ruined, almost instantaneously, our valuable and widely extended commerce.

The evils designed to be remedied by this measure, which thus ruined our commerce and destroyed our shipping, were comparatively trifling. Of our ten thousand vessels not more than an average of one hundred and fifty were annually captured, and of these one-third were released. Sound policy dictated the increase of our army and navy, the strengthening of our fortifications, and a temporizing course no longer than the preparation of our resources for the offensive demanded. Had we pursued this policy, it is certain that both France and England would ultimately have indemnified us in preference to seeing us resort to hostilities. By the embargo, on the other hand, we not only cut off our valuable commerce with England herself, but transferred to her our valuable trade with China, the Indies, Spain, Portugal, Sweden, Norway, and Russia. More than this, the commerce of the seas, which we so recklessly resigned, England took possession of at once, anticipating in this way a more than ample indemnity for the expenses of the war which we subsequently declared against her. The declaration of war in 1812 was but a consequence of the policy which passed the embargo act. The conduct of the war, although in many particulars creditable to the bravery and patriotism of the people, upon the whole reflects shame upon the government, which being recklessly engaged—without an army, navy, fortifications, officers, or credit—in hostilities with a great power, ignominiously suffered the national capital to be captured, imposed a burdensome public debt upon the republic, and found itself forced to end the war without the enforcement of a single concession from its adversary, or the settlement of a single contested point. Jefferson, who after his term as President expired, continued to direct the policy of his party, is largely responsible for the disastrous consequences of the embargo and the war. His prejudices against England and his passions as a partisan misled his judgment. When free from the influence of such feelings, he was capable of taking enlarged and liberal views of our foreign policy, as is shown by the following facts :

1. Jefferson is entitled to the credit of having prepared the way for our territorial expansion, by the precedent which he established in the purchase of Louisiana.

2. He was the first of our statesmen to comprehend the vast importance to American interests of the inter-oceanic canal. In 1787–1789, while he acted as our diplomatic representative at Paris, he carried on a correspondence with Mr. Carmichael, the American chargé at Madrid, urging him to obtain as much information as possible in regard to the surveys made by the Spanish government, for a canal across the Central American isthmus. In a letter to Mr. Carmichael, dated Paris, May 27th, 1788, Mr. Jefferson says in reference to the matter, "This report is to me a vast desideratum for reasons *political* and philosophical."

3. If not the author of the Monroe doctrine, he is entitled to the credit of having had an important share in putting it into shape by his advice to Mr. Monroe, contained in his letter to him dated Monticello, October 24th, 1823.

4. He favored the acquisition of Cuba by the United States. On the 3d of June, 1823, he wrote to President Monroe in reference to that island, saying, "Certainly her addition to our confederacy is exactly what is wanting to round our power as a nation to the point of its utmost interest." He afterward wrote to the same person that the "annexation of Cuba would fill up the measure of our political well-being."

The immediate result of Mr. Monroe's consultations with Mr. Jefferson was the promulgation of the *Monroe doctrine*, which terminated an inglorious epoch of the history of the country. Mr. Wharton,. in his introduction to the "American State Trials," refers with just pride to the Monroe declaration in the following terms:

"At last the United States, which fifty years ago could hardly keep its central territory from being carried away under its very eyes, announced to Europe that it would consider any foreign interference in the affairs of the American continent as a cause of war ; and Europe listened and acquiesced."

The Clayton-Bulwer treaty again brought the consistency of our diplomacy into question. Six days. after the signing of the treaty which secured to us California, and gave us command of the Pacific coast. of North America, England seized on the territory at the mouth of the San Juan for the purpose of se-

6

curing the control of the transit route across the Central American isthmus, in connection with the canal projects of Prince Louis Napoleon, then under consideration in London. The seizure was a clear infringement of the Monroe doctrine, and should have been resisted emphatically. It really led only to the negotiation of the so-called Clayton-Bulwer treaty, or, more properly speaking, Convention of 1850. This convention contains the following remarkable concession :

" The governments of the United States and Great Britain hereby declare that neither the one nor the other will obtain or maintain for itself any exclusive control over said ship canal ; agreeing that neither will ever erect or maintain any fortifications commanding the same, or in the vicinity thereof, or occupy, or fortify, or colonize, or assume, or exercise any dominion over Nicaragua, Costa Rica, the Mosquito coast, or any part of Central America ; nor will either make use of any protection which either affords, or may afford, or any alliance which either has or may have to or with any state or people for the purpose of erecting or maintaining any such fortifications, or of occupying, fortifying, or colonizing Nicaragua, Costa Rica, the Mosquito coast, or any part of Central America, or of assuming or exercising dominion over the same ; . . ."

This convention was ratified through the influence

of the administration, notwithstanding the strong protest of many influential senators. A senator so conservative as Mr. Wilson of Massachusetts, subsequently in the Senate openly advocated its abrogation. This may not be required, the convention having in fact abrogated itself. But we must protect our own interests at all hazards, and whether that can be done without the formal revocation of the Clayton-Bulwer treaty, as proposed by Vice-President Wilson, is a question which the future must decide.

It should be our policy, not to prevent the construction of a canal at Panama or elsewhere, but to secure the *control* of any such canal beyond peradventure. We do not seek to drive foreign enterprise and capital from this continent, but to provide against their being used to make subject American interests to foreign domination. It is not necessary for us probably to seize upon the territory to be pierced by the canal, but it is necessary for us to establish ourselves on such vantage ground as shall secure our safety against local revolutions, broken treaties, foreign interventions, and all the complications sure to spring from the relations of a vast corporation to a weak and unstable government.

We must plant our flag firmly and permanently on either side of the isthmus. Whether the enterprise of M. de Lesseps fails or succeeds, such action

on our part is absolutely necessary to protect the
canal if a canal be constructed by us, and to domi-
nate it if constructed by foreigners. We have suffered matters to drift too long and to our grave
detriment. Our neglect confronts us with the alter-
native of a foreign war in the near future, or of
the immediate occupation of commanding naval
positions on either Isthmian sea. The Monroe doctrine embodies the only true foreign policy which
this government has ever had. It is founded on the
highest principles of justice and of self-preservation.
To these considerations all others must bow.

Passing over our foreign relations between 1850 and
1861, we come to the momentous period of the civil
war, an event which found Mr. Seward in charge of
our foreign office. This was a circumstance of fortunate significance for the welfare of a country which
has never adopted the wise policy of preparing men
for diplomatic careers by special training.

It was the patriotic and instructive insight of this
eminent statesman which enabled him to perform
the duties of Secretary of State during the most try-
ing period in the entire history of our foreign relations, with a success which earned for him a high
and enduring fame.

The firmness, persistence, and complete success
with which he enforced the Monroe doctrine against
the French invaders of Mexico affords the most con-

spicuous proof of this. The negotiation of a treaty for the purchase of the island of St. Thomas as a naval station followed the termination of the civil war. It was the conviction of Mr. Seward that the naval and commercial interests of the nation demanded the acquisition of insular possessions in all quarters of the globe. The Senate, unfortunately, was not prepared to accept his enlightened and sagacious views, and the treaty was rejected. With the treaty for the purchase of Alaska, Mr. Seward was more fortunate. Yet, popular as that measure was, its full import was not generally understood at the time of the purchase. The Secretary of State had acted with reference to very remote results. The immediate benefits of the annexation of Alaska, great as they were, were to him but of little consequence compared with the fact that the treaty looked to the extension of our dominion over the whole of North America.

This expansive idea was not a new one to Mr. Seward. As early as 1856, in a debate in the Senate of the United States, he said:

"We are the center of one system, an American one; Great Britain is the center of another, an European one. Almost in spite of ourselves, we are steadily extending and increasing our control over these continents. Notwithstanding her tenacity, she is constantly losing her dominion here. This is within the order of nature. It was for three hundred years the business of European nations to colonize, discipline, and educate American nations. It is now the business of those nations to govern themselves. The decline of European power here practically began with the fall of Canada out of the control in 1763. It has steadily continued, until now only some relics possessing little vitality remain. Without any war on our part, Great Britain will wisely withdraw and disappear from this hemisphere within a quarter of a century, or at least within half a century."

The germ of the Alaska treaty is to be found in these remarks. Its import is clearly indicated in the speech of Mr. Seward at Sitka, in 1869, on his return from his voyage around the world. Referring to the resources of the Pacific coast, he said :

"The entire region of Oregon, Washington Territory, British Columbia, and Alaska, seems thus destined to become a ship-yard for the supply of all nations. I do not forget on this occasion that British Columbia belongs within a foreign jurisdiction. *That circumstance does not materially affect my calculations.* British Columbia, by whomsoever possessed, must be governed in conformity with the interests of her people, and of society upon the American continent. If that territory shall be so governed, there will be no ground of complaint anywhere. If it shall be governed so as to conflict with the interests of the inhabitants of that territory, *we all can easily foresee what will happen in that case.*"

The crowning glory, however, of Mr. Seward's diplomatic career was his negotiation of the treaty of Darien, the sixth article of which embodied provisions securing to the United States absolute control of the proposed inter-oceanic canal at the Darien crossing. It is true this treaty was rejected by Colombia through French and English influences. It nevertheless established a precedent which must be followed wherever and within whatever jurisdiction the canal may be finally built.

The article in question provided that:

"As soon as the canal, together with its dependencies and appurtenances, shall be constructed, the inspection, possession, direction, and government of it will belong to the United States of America, and it will be exercised by that government; that of the United States of Colombia having the power, after the exchange of this convention, of keeping a permanent commission of agents, with the right to inspect the respective operations, to ascertain the tonnage of vessels, to examine the accounts, and to report thereupon to the government of the United States of Colombia, but not to interfere in the supervision, government, management, direction, and administration of the canal."

The entire document is worthy of careful study on account of the thoroughly American spirit which pervades it. It is a grand practical commentary on the Monroe doctrine. No administration in any future convention with the local authorities of the isthmus will ever venture to depart from the principles embodied in the Darien treaty, nor must any European government hereafter be permitted to disregard, in spirit or in fact, this distinct declaration of our policy.

Mr. Seward had the sagacity to perceive that any corporation strong enough to build a canal on the isthmus, would virtually own the weak and distracted republic of Colombia, which would soon become a mere province of the nation granting the charter to such a corporation. We are now brought face to face with these anticipated dangers.

A French corporation, organized for the construction of this great work, and now on the ground in active prosecution of the requisite preliminary details, will soon govern the United States of Colombia from the banks of the Seine. The time has come for the authorities at Washington to announce that the control of any canal to be built at Darien, Nicaragua, or elsewhere, by whomsoever built, and whatever the nationality of its corporators, belongs, and must belong, exclusively to the United States of America.

Such an announcement would fitly mark the beginning of a new era in our foreign policy, in which, without departing from the precepts of Washington with regard to alliances, our power shall make itself felt so effectually as to protect those vast continental interests, which it is our privilege and our duty to supervise. In this matter we have both right and tradition, reason and expediency with us. We are assuming no new ground. The principles applicable to the case are traditional. The proposed canal will be a main artery of our colossal coastwise trade. Its route runs within the prospective bounds of our republic ; we are bound by the teachings of experience, and by all our political and commercial interests, to take efficient means now, at the outset, to secure it. The sentiments of the American people on the subject admit of no question. The emergency is here at our doors. It calls for prompt and energetic action. We should prepare for all contingencies at once by greatly strengthening our navy, and by establishing naval stations at commanding positions upon the Caribbean and the Pacific sides of the isthmus. These are measures demanded not only by the urgency of the inter-oceanic canal question, but by common sense and a rational regard to our political and commercial interests everywhere.

COLONIZATION AND PROVINCIAL POSSESSIONS CONSIDERED IN RELATION TO THE INTERESTS OF THE UNITED STATES.

VENICE, Carthage, Greece, and Rome all owed their political greatness largely to their colonies. The colonial system was a favorite method for the defense of military conquests and the extension of the limits of commerce. Among the Greeks, colonies were often established by those who wished to escape the tyranny of factions at home. Rome in her colonial system founded that wise policy, by which her territorial jurisdiction and her pre-eminence were maintained. Her colonies were the outposts of her conquests, and the disseminators of her language and laws to the remotest regions of the empire. Unquestionably, all the great European powers have owed much of their strength and wealth to their colonial and provincial acquisitions.

To sustain this assertion by examples would be merely to give a list of great sovereignties from the beginning of history down to the days of the world-wide empire of that dominion, "which has dotted over the surface of the globe with her possessions and military posts; whose morning drum-beat, following the sun and keeping company with the hours, circles the earth with one continuous and unbroken strain of the martial airs of England." The history of British colonization is familiar. Great Britain's colonies cover one-sixth of land surface of the globe, and include nearly an equal portion of its population. Of the territory of the world available for colonization, about eighty per cent. now belongs to the Anglo-Saxon race. The relative importance of the colonial interests of the various nations of the globe is shown by the following table:

Powers.	Colonial Area, Sq. Miles.	Colonial Population.
Great Britain	8,015,028	204,535,000
France	247,642	4,019,500
Spain	120,703	8,584,000
Portugal	690,451	3,618,000
Holland	681,436	24,110,000
Denmark	34,140	47,500
Sweden	8	2,900

The colonies of Great Britain have not only extended the blessings of English laws and English liberty throughout the globe, but have also largely contributed to the wealth of the mother country, and it is chiefly due to the magnificent contributions of these dependencies that England has advanced from an insignificant kingdom in the days of her Norman sovereigns, to the commanding position she holds among the nations. Her numerous possessions have had an important influence upon her internal economy. They have opened an outlet for her surplus population, fostered and enlarged her commerce, and maintained the stability of her government. It is not to be contended that a similar policy is or ever will be wise or appropriate for the United States, nor that any general schemes of conquest or annexation should be encouraged by our people. But we have reached a stage in our national growth which may render it expedient to strengthen ourselves by judicious acquisitions of external dependencies, and we should seek expansion only as an incident to, and in furtherance of, strength and self-protection. At the opening of the present century, it was earnestly debated in the Senate of the United States whether it would be safe to acquire territory on the west bank of the Mississippi River. It was then contended that such an extension of our territory would be dangerous, and that it would be wise to make the Alleghanies the barrier beyond which we ought not to pass. At a later day more liberal views prevailed, and it was thought we might safely venture to establish one tier of States west of the Mississippi. The expedient was then resorted to of establishing an Indian Territory in perpetuity all along our western border, for the express purpose of preventing the establishment of any new States in that direction! The extension of our dominion to the shores of the Pacific was then thought to be entirely improbable. Jefferson, in a letter to Mr. Astor, written in 1813, in reference to the settlement on the Columbia River in Oregon, calls it the "germ of a great, free, and independent empire on that side of our continent; and even so late as in 1848, Daniel Webster himself thought it impracticable to govern the States upon the Pacific from this side of the continent. In a speech in Faneuil Hall, on the 7th of November of that year, he said, "and now let me ask if there be any sensible man in the whole United States who will say for a moment that when fifty or a hundred thousand persons of this description, Americans mainly, but all Anglo-Saxons, shall find themselves on the shores of the Pacific Ocean, they will long consent to be under the rules of the American Congress, or British Parliament. They will raise the standard for themselves, and they ought to do it." Two years afterward Mr. Webster admitted that his apprehensions had

not been realized.* The truth is that the telegraph
and the steam engine have silently revolutionized
the conditions of political power throughout the
world.

The acquisition of California and Oregon, and
their admission into the Union, greatly enlarged the
views of our statesmen, and Mr. Everett, Secretary
of State in 1852, in his letter on the tripartite
treaty, took the ground that we would *not relin-
quish the privilege of taking possession of any portion whatever of this continent.* Speaking with
special reference to Central America, Vice-President
Wilson said in the Senate, in 1856, "I have no sympathy with the policy that would extend the boundaries of the republic by lawless violence, but I have
faith in democratic institutions. I believe that
wherever the jurisdiction of this country extends
on this continent, the interests of humanity will be
ultimately promoted by it. Agreeing with the doctrine laid down by Mr. Everett in his admirable letter upon the tripartite treaty, I would never bind
ourselves by any treaty that we would not annex, if
we and the people who live in the country desire it,
any portion of this continent. For myself I can
never vote to admit a foot of territory into this
Union where the great doctrine of the Declaration

---

* Jefferson's Writings, Vol. VI., p. 55; Boston Daily Advertiser, Nov.
9th, 1848; Webster's Works, Vol. II., p. 526.

of Independence, that all men are created free, is denied ; *but wherever freedom and free institutions can follow the American flag, I am ready to annex that portion of the continent*, if it can be accomplished honorably, peacefully, and in harmony with the people who are to come to us." Such were the views entertained by so conservative a senator as Mr. Wilson prior to the civil war. That event did not check the advance of public sentiment, but on the contrary, accelerated it. In 1861, Mr. Lincoln entered into an agreement on the part of the United States with an American citizen owning a part of the Isthmus of Panama, for the colonization there of the recently emancipated slaves, and Congress placed at his disposal an appropriation of six hundred thousand dollars to carry the agreement into effect. It is understood that this contract is a subsisting obligation, and can be made use of whenever the freedmen choose to claim its performance by the government. The war had scarcely closed when the nation was found willing to sanction the purchase of Alaska. As this is the first instance in which we have acquired territory divided by an intervening foreign state from our previous possessions, the precedent is one of importance as indicating that in future our annexations are not to be restricted to contiguous territory, nor prevented by dissimilarity of race and language, if otherwise desirable. The

treaty for the purchase of Alaska was ratified by the
Senate while Mr. Sumner was chairman of the com-
mittee on foreign relations. It is well known that he
zealously advocated its ratification. His familiarity
with European politics, his thorough knowledge of
ancient and modern history, his love of broad statesmanship, gave him rare qualifications as a wise
adviser in regard to this new measure of national
policy. He had, moreover, studied with special
care the problem of our territorial expansion, and in
the last years of his life, as a consequence of his
thoughtful consideration of the subject, the ultimate
absorption of the entire continent of North America
by our republic, was regarded by him as not at all
improbable. In advocating the ratification of the
Alaska treaty, he said, "The present treaty is a
visible step in the occupation of the whole North
American continent. As such it will be recognized
by the world, and accepted by the American people.
But the treaty involves something more. By it we
dismiss one more monarch from this continent. One
by one they have retired ; first France ; then Spain ;
then France again ; and now Russia ; all giving way
to that absorbing unity declared in the national
motto, *E Pluribus Unum.*" Let no one suppose
that Mr. Sumner was carried away by mere ora-
torical fervor. He followed the footsteps of John
Adams, who, writing in London on the 1st of Janu-

ary, 1787, predicted that our republic would spread over the "northern part of that whole quarter of the globe." Thus, says Sumner, "even at that early day was the destiny of the republic manifest." The prophecy was a sound philosophical deduction from the history of the growth of empires. As a general rule the acquisition of territory has been the normal rule of national development, and the sign of national health and vigor. Such acquisitions must be regarded as the law of the being of a nation like ours. Mr. Sumner, in his speech on the Alaska treaty, very properly laid stress upon the measure as one that would extend our dominion. Referring to the fact that "few are so cold or philosophical as to regard with insensibility the widening of the bounds of country," he recites with pride the history of our territorial acquisitions, beginning with the purchase of Louisiana in 1803, and traces to its natural and beneficent source the universal desire of nations for territorial expansion, in the following paragraph:

"The passion for acquisition, which is so strong in the individual, is not less strong in the community. A nation seeks an outlying territory as an individual seeks an outlying farm. The passion shows itself constantly. France, passing into Africa, has annexed Algeria. Spain set her face in the same direction, but without the same success. There are

7

two great powers with which annexation has become a habit. One is Russia, which from the time of Peter the Great has been moving her flag forward in every direction, so that on every side her limits have been extended. Even now the report comes that she is lifting her southern landmarks in Asia, so as to carry her boundary to India. The other annexationist is Great Britain, which from time to time adds another province to her Indian dominion. If our country has occasionally added to her dominion, she has only yielded to the universal passion, although I do not forget that the late Theodore Parker was accustomed to say that above all people the Anglo-Saxons were remarkable for greed of land. It was land, not gold, that aroused the Anglo-Saxon phlegm. I doubt, however, if the passion be stronger with us than with others, except perhaps that in a community where all participate in government, the national sentiments are more active. It is common to the human family. There are few anywhere who could hear of a considerable accession of territory obtained peacefully and honestly, without a pride of country, even if at certain moments the judgment hesitated. With an increased size on the map, there is an increased consciousness of strength, and the heart of the citizen throbs anew as he traces the extending line." The predictions of our leading statesmen thus clearly point to the annexation of territory in the future. It is not too soon to consider the policy which shall direct those acquisitions. British statesmen themselves admit that the absorption of British America by the United States is but a question of time. Mr. Bright, in a speech delivered on the 18th of December, 1862, said:

"I have a far other and far brighter vision before my gaze. It may be but a vision, but I will cherish it. I see one vast confederation stretching from the frozen north in unbroken line to the glowing south, and from the wild billows of the Atlantic westward to the calmer waters of the Pacific main: and I see one people, and one law, and one language, and one faith, and over all that wide continent the home of freedom and a refuge for the oppressed of every race and of every clime."

Turning to Mexico, we find her greatest historian virtually admitting that his country is destined to disappear from the map, except as a subordinate part of the great republic of the north. Alaman says, "Mexico will be without doubt a land of prosperity from its natural advantages, but it will not be so for the races which now inhabit it." In 1823 Mr. Jefferson said, in regard to Cuba, "Her addition to our confederacy is exactly what is wanting to round out our power as a nation to the point of its utmost interest," a sentiment which has since been concurred in by many of our statesmen. The treaty for the purchase of the island of St. Thomas was hastily rejected on narrow and unwise grounds; and that for the acquisition of Santo Domingo, so creditable to the diplomacy of Grant's administration, was defeated by the animosity of a faction, and not for sound reasons of public policy. So far then as insular or isthmian possessions are concerned, we are not restrained from acquiring them either by precedents, or the precepts of our wisest statesmen. There are many localities which would be valuable to us, either as naval stations or for commercial reasons, and they will doubtless become our dependencies, especially when our long-depressed shipping interests shall have been revived by proper congressional legislation. As to Central America, the plainest principles of sound national policy dictate that the region which contains the gate of the Pacific should be a dependency of our republic, whose vital interests, present and prospective, are so intimately concerned with the construction and control of an inter-oceanic canal. Aside from other grave public considerations, the fact that the canal will be the connecting link in our immense coastwise trade from Maine to Alaska, imposes upon us at least the necessity for its military and naval control. The smallest beginnings in the right direction may result in a most splendid consummation. Lord Mahon, in his history of England, forcibly says that the story of

the establishment of the British Indian Empire sur-
passes in marvelousness "the prodigies wrought by
spells or talismans, by the lamp of Aladdin, or
the seals of Solomon." These magnificent results
sprang from a feeble trading establishment, which
under the wise care of the mother country grew into
empire. Mr. Wood, in his recent work on the
British colonies, says : "In Hong-Kong we find a
small barren island, which at the time of its cession
to Britain was inhabited only by a few handfuls of
fishermen, now crowded with tens of thousands of
Chinese, who have crossed from the mainland because they knew that under British rule they would
be free from oppressive taxation, would be governed
by just laws, and would be able to carry on a thriv-
ing and profitable trade. And so in the once uninhab-
ited island of Singapore, we see a motley population attracted from China, the Malay Peninsula, and
India, by a similar cause." The mere establishment
of naval stations upon the isthmus would be the sure
forerunner of such a colony. Protection under the
American flag would open up to our enterprising
citizens a country rivaling the wealth of the East.
The riotous and ungarnered luxuriance of that won-
derful and almost unknown land, under the guiding
hand of civilized husbandry and Anglo-Saxon enterprise, would contribute its lavish quota of wealth,
not to us only, but to the world. It would at once

give us new and commanding commercial relations
with South America and Russia, with China, Japan,
and the islands of the Pacific. Our trade would
increase with the extension of our authority, and
ultimately become the chief source of our national
wealth and prosperity. Why should we not have
our naval stations in every sea, and harbors of our
own? Why not have our own Hong-Kongs and
Singapores? Did any sound maxim of national
policy require us to reject proffered protectorates
over such valuable possessions as the Samoan Islands and Santo Domingo? There are weighty reasons in the social condition of the United States
which render it expedient that a more liberal policy
of territorial expansion should obtain. Free schools
and popular education have introduced peculiar and
difficult social problems. A large class of persons
with educated tastes and habits, which their financial
circumstances do not allow them to gratify, born to
social and political aspirations they cannot hope to
realize, owing to excessive competition, may hope to
find their opportunities in colonial enterprise. The
effects of this condition of things appear in the
numbers who crowd the learned professions; in the
throngs who are always pressing for admission into
the civil service of the nation, and in the fact that
every department of intellectual work is overcrowd-
ed. The same trouble felt in England is thus re-

ferred to by Earl Stanhope, in his history of the reign of Queen Anne. "At present there are few things more distressing to any one who desires to see general prosperity and content prevail, than to find start up, whenever any opening in any career is made known, not one or two, but ten or twenty candidates. Every one of these twenty may be in every case perfectly well qualified to fill the place that he seeks, yet only one can be chosen. What is then to become of the nineteen?" The acquisition of insular, transmarine, South American and Central American possessions would have a beneficial influence upon our national politics, by enlarging and liberalizing the views of our statesmen, and by tranquilizing our domestic affairs with external subjects of consideration. The policy above indicated concerns itself only with such peaceful acquisitions as would inevitably result from the promulgation of the fact of our willingness to admit within our jurisdiction such petty and distracted commonwealths as might voluntarily seek peace and security under our flag. The admission of a great foreign power upon soil contiguous to our own presents the question whether the paramount demands of national protection do not require the forestalling of such occupation by occupation. The law of private self-preservation, which would forbid a man to suffer his neighbor to found a powder mill next door to his house, extends to national affairs. Some occult reason, perhaps beyond explanation, has made it evident that the mixed races of Central America are incapable of successful self-government. The fairest regions of the globe have, since the discovery of this continent, been practically closed to the legitimate exercise of commercial privileges and the arts of peace. It is a fact that the Latin races have never been prosperous colonists nor practical republicans. These petty states, as republics, have belied the name, by constant internal strife marked by cruelty and bloodshed. Now, under the name of republics, they have been hot-beds of license, and now, under the rule of dictators, strongholds of tyranny. Throughout their entire history, these states have offered premiums for the establishment of monarchies upon this continent. They are standing menaces to our own safety. When it is considered that under a strong but constitutional government, these states, which contain within their borders the very gardens of the earth, might be opened to the peaceful commerce and industries of the world, that the happiness and prosperity of their own inhabitants might be secured—when it is considered that from the gloom of semi-barbarism they might be ushered into the sunlight of civilization, it requires no subtle casuistry to justify their redemption from *themselves* if need be. If to all this we add the paramount demands of our own self-protection, and the prophecies of the fathers of our republic become to us not only predictions, but *commands.*

THE UNITED STATES SHOULD CONTROL THE INTER-OCEANIC CANAL.

THE consideration of foreign affairs has been, with our public men, a matter of secondary importance for a long time past, as compared with domestic questions. Public sentiment, however, in the United States under the guidance of enlightened statesmanship, in which our most conservative statesmen have participated, anticipates the final absorption of the North American continent within the bounds of the United States.

This sentiment, as Sumner remarks, had its origin in opposition to kingly dominion in the New World. Our revolutionary ancestors were, he says, "Roman in character, and turned to Roman lessons. With a cynical austerity the early Cato said that kings were 'carnivorous animals,' and at his instance the Roman Senate decreed that no king should be allowed within the gates of the city. A kindred sentiment, with less austerity of form, has been received from our fathers ; *but our city can be nothing less*

*than the North American continent, with its gates
on all the surrounding seas."*

And in the same spirit of enlightened patriotism
Webster, in a vivid portrayal of the destiny of our
country, had previously used Homer's beautiful description of the border of the shield of Achilles :

> " Now the broad shield complete, the artist crowned
>   With his last hand, and poured the ocean round ;
>   In living silver seemed the waves to roll,
>   And beat the buckler's verge, and bound the whole."

But while the aspirations and hopes alike of our
people and our statesmen point to this wide ultimate
extension of American dominion, it is not strange
that European powers should contemplate with apprehension every step toward such an ascendancy.
France, and particularly the Imperial party in
France, has for the last twenty years been active in
plans and efforts to check the territorial expansion
of the United States. She has assumed the direction
of this aggressive work, as being the leading Latin
power.

The avowed purpose of the French invasion of
Mexico during the late civil war was to curb Anglo-
Saxon progress beyond the borders of Texas ; and it
was openly declared in the famous letter of Louis
Napoleon to General Forey, that his object in
founding an empire in Mexico was the establishment

of the power of the Latin race on this continent, as a counterpoise to the Anglo-Saxon dominion. The French newspapers of that period may be profitably studied for the light they throw on the designs of France in this quarter of the globe. An exultant article published in the "France" in 1864, upon the successful establishment of the empire in Mexico, thus concludes :

"Lastly, French interests must there find guarantees and particular advantages, which cannot fail to excite attention. There has been created on the other side of the Atlantic, by the victories of our soldiers, an empire which owes its existence to us; which the bonds of the most cordial friendship, and of the most legitimate gratitude must unite us to; which will give fresh strength to the straightforward influences of our policy in the New World, and open the unexplored treasures of its vast territory to French commerce and industry."

Such are still the sentiments of French statesmen and of the leaders of French thought. Is the "policy in the New World," which failed under the guiding hand of Louis Napoleon, to be made a splendid success under de Lesseps? The inter-oceanic canal project of M. de Lesseps—although in its inception urged as a great international and "fraternal" enterprise—has been from the first thoroughly French, and designed for the promotion of French interests alone. The canal is to be built under a French charter, and by a preponderance of French capital. The concession from Colombia is owned by a French company. The amount of capital required to build the canal is so great, relatively to the financial resources of Colombia, that the corporation owning it would be much greater than the state itself. French troops must sooner or later protect it. It will be administered by French officials, who will schedule and impose tolls upon the commerce passing through it. More than two-thirds of that commerce at the outset must be the commerce of the United States of America. All the numerous and important litigated questions as to maritime and national and international rights and liabilities, concerning the transit of passengers and freight, must be adjudicated either at Bogota, virtually under French influence, or at Paris itself.

A correspondent of the New York *World*, reporting a recent interview at Panama with M. de Lesseps, gives us his plans and expectations in this respect. In his own words,

"M. de Lesseps says that all questions regarding the canal, its tonnage, and management, with whomsoever they may arise, will be decided by the French courts, as in the case of Suez. The local Colombian courts will not give the company guarantee enough of justice, while the French courts are worthy of all confidence. In important matters, then, they will have arbitration—in matters in which the Colombian government may be concerned. All this is to be decided by the articles of association. But one thing is sure—every question about the management of the canal must be brought up in France, not in Colombia. Both M. de Lesseps and (which is the same thing) M. Bionne, the general superintendent, and really the 'man behind the throne,' who is a clever lawyer, insist on this point.

"I asked particularly whether he did not think that this proposed recourse to the French courts, on matters which in the regular way should be adjudicated in the local courts, was not an infringement of the sovereignty of the Republic of Colombia. M. de Lesseps cannot see any derogation of the perfect independence of that republic in what he proposes to do. The local courts do not give guarantees enough, and the regulation of jurisdiction is to be fixed by an arrangement with the Colombian authorities."

If, in addition to these commercial and economical considerations, we take into account the political consequences of the construction of the canal under foreign auspices, the argument for the permanent and effectual *neutralization* of the project by our own government becomes irresistible. Treaty negotiations will not answer. The occupation of commanding naval and military positions upon the isthmus alone will accomplish the purpose. Colombia is destined to become a French province. A transatlantic foreign power, established as a neighbor, will control the most important channel of our immense coastwise trade. A foreign nation will at any time be able, if hostile, to close that channel to us in case of war with any great power. In time of peace we could doubtless secure favorable conditions for the passage of our shipping, but war would place us at the mercy of the great foreign corporation virtually owning the United States of Colombia.

M. de Lesseps, commenting on the Burnside resolution, said, "he had always been of the opinion that the canal should be independent of the control of any and every foreign government." Whatever countenance our government may have given to this idea in the ill-advised Clayton-Bulwer convention, the Darien treaty, a subsequent and far more deliberate and well-considered instrument, more truly formulates the purpose of the American people. It is true that, induced by French and English influences, the United States of Colombia declined to consummate that treaty. It, notwithstanding, embodies the principles to which the United States will henceforth adhere. The Senate of the United States was influenced solely by the supposition that the canal was about to be built by an American corporation,

when it ratified in 1850 the Clayton-Bulwer convention. Our interest in the canal is of such an exceptional character as compared with the interest of
any other nation, or of all other nations, that this
circumstance must necessarily control our action.
Opening to us as it does new facilities for trade between our eastern and western coast, over the entire
line from Maine to Alaska, and placing within easy
reach the western coast of South America, the
shores of Asia, and the islands of the Pacific, we
must possess over it a control beyond the power
of stipulations to give, or of their violation to de-
stroy. Its joint supervision with us by any foreign
power or combination of powers, or even its guaran-
teed neutrality, would leave these vast interests beyond our own grasp and at the mercy of the uncer-
tain events of European politics. Our acquiescence
in the stipulations of a convention to guarantee the
neutrality of the Mississippi, would not be more absurd or weak than was our acceptance of the Clayton-
Bulwer convention. Louis Napoleon, in his letter to
General Forey, said, "It is not the interest of France
that America should grasp the whole Gulf of Mexico, rule thence the Antilles as well as South America, and be the sole dispenser of the products of
the New World." Could words more clearly sug-
gest at once our policy and our danger ? The efforts
in which our government is now engaged, through its

consular and diplomatic agents, to extend our commerce have given it a new impetus. With the attractions of a vast commercial prosperity in the near future beckoning us on, we cannot look with indif-. ference upon the attempts of a great power to gain control of the only water communications between our Atlantic and Pacific coasts. The *Bulletin du Canal Interoceanique*, the official organ of M. de Lesseps, portrays in glowing terms the rich commercial rewards of this future monument to French enterprise. In a strain more inspiring still to the imagination of the patriotic Frenchman it prophesies a great increase of the "prestige" of France, "one of the best conditions of its commercial growth." Its martial and commercial enthusiasm intimately blending, it points to the fact that "England gives proof of this, and her constant efforts on all sides to maintain her prestige, even at the expense of painful and costly wars, tell us plainly enough the value she attaches to it—she whose policy is, above all things, commercial." Here are no traces of that fraternal, disinterested spirit by which the distinguished engineer of the Suez Canal would persuade us he is actuated in his so-called "international enterprise." French *prestige* is the golden fleece which lures the modern Jason to the setting sun, albeit through "painful and costly wars." Let us at once admire his patriotic zeal, do justice to his genius, and be-

8

ware of the "painful and costly wars." In 1523 Charles V. enjoined Cortez to search thoroughly for the "strait into the Indian Ocean." How thoroughly the great explorer appreciated the importance of the undertaking is shown in his reply. Referring to the anticipated discovery, he says :

"It would render the King of Spain master of so many kingdoms that he might consider himself *Lord of the World.*"

APPENDIX.

A chronological list of the efforts to secure inter-oceanic transits across the isthmus or the continent of Central America.

1528. Antonio Galvao proposed a scheme to Charles V. for opening up a route between the two oceans.

1534. Instructions of Charles V. to Cortez to seek such a route.

1551. Gomara, author of the "History of the Indies," proposed three routes, including Nicaragua.

1567. Antonelli sent by Philip II. to explore Nicaragua.

1701. Patterson's "Four Passes" published.

1745. Proposals of citizens of Oaxaca for opening the Tehuantepec route.

1774. The Tehuantepec route explored by Cramer.

1780. The English attempt to seize the Nicaragua route for England. Nelson serving in the expedition.

1781. Exploration of the San Juan River (Nicaragua) by Galisteo.

1797. Miranda's proposals to William Pitt.

1804. Humboldt's nine routes proposed.

1814. A decree of the Spanish Cortes passed for opening a canal across Tehuantepec.

1824. Exploration of Tehuantepec by Orbegozo.

1825. Grant by the Government of New Granada to Baron de Thierry for a canal at Panama.

1827. Surveys made under Bolivar.

1830. A company formed in Holland to open the Nicaragua route.

1836. Mission of Col. Biddle to Central America.

1838. Baily's survey of Nicaragua.

1842. Garay's survey of Tehuantepec.

1843. Garella's survey of the Panama route.

1845. Proposals made to Louis Napoleon by Nicaragua to open a canal.

1849. Dr. Cullen's explorations.

1849. A canal charter to the American, Atlantic and Pacific Canal Company of New York, granted by Nicaragua.

1851. Col. Childs's survey of the Nicaragua route.

1853. Survey of the Atrato route for Mr. Kelley.

1854. Survey of the Honduras route by Squier.

1855. Panama Railroad.

1858. Trautwine's survey of the Honduras route.

1858. M. Belly obtained a grant from Nicaragua for canal.

1858. Survey of the Atrato route by Lieut. Craven, *et al.*

1861. Bourdial's expedition.

1864. Captain Pim's expedition.

1865. Remy de Puydt's expedition.

1866. Sacharma and Flachat's expeditions.

1868-9. The Ayon-Chevalier contract with Nicaragua.

1870-3. Reports by Selfridge—Darien route.

1872. Report by Captain Shufeldt on the Tehuantepec route.

1872-3. Report by Lull on the Nicaragua route from Grey-town to Brito.

1872-3. A canal contract granted by Costa Rica to Henry Meiggs of Peru.

1875. Re-survey of the Selfridge route by Lieut. Collins.

1875. Reconnoissance of the Panama route by Com. E. P. Lull.

1876-7. The French reconnoissance under the direction of Lieut. Bonaparte Wyse.

1879. The Paris conference under M. de Lesseps.

List of proposed routes for canals and roads across the Central American isthmus, as given in the report of Admiral Davis to Congress in 1866.

CANALS.

I........................	1. Tehuantepec, by the Coatzacoalcos and Chicapa.
II........................	2. Honduras.
	3. R. San Carlos, G. de Nicoya.
	4. R. Niño, Tempisque, G. de Nicoya.
	5. R. Sapoa B. Salinas.
III.. *River San Juan de Nicaragua. Lake Nicaragua.*	6. San Juan del Sur.
	7. Brito.
	8. R. Tamarinda.
L. Managua.	9. P. Realejo.
	10. B. Fonseca.
	11. Gorgona, Panama.
R. Chagres.	12. Trinidad, Caymito.
IV..Panama	13. Navy Bay, R. Chagres, R. Bonito, R. Bernardo.
	14. San Blas, R. Chepo.
	15. B. Caledonia, G. San Miguel.
	16. Rs. Arguia, Paya, Tuyra, G. San Miguel.
V.. Darien	17. R. Napipi, Cupica.
Rio Atrato.	18. R. Truando, Kelly's I.
	19. R. Tuyra, G. Urabá or R. Atrato.

ROADS.

I.—Coatzacoalcos, Tehuantepec.
II.—B. Honduras to G. of Fonseca.
III.—R. San Juan, Nicaragua, Managua, G. of Fonseca.
IV.—Port Limon to Caldera, Costa Rica.
V.—Chiriqui inlet to Golfo Dulce.
VI.—Aspinwall, Panama (railroad finished).
VII.—Gorgon B., Realejo.   } Nicaragua.
VIII.—Gorgon B., San Juan del Sur. }

www.ingramcontent.com/pod-product-compliance
Lightning Source LLC
Chambersburg PA
CBHW030630270326
41927CB00007B/1388